Critical Acclaim for Books
By Gen and Kelly Tanabe

"Upbeat, well-organized and engaging."
—*Publishers Weekly*

"Helpful, well-organized guide, with copies of actual letters and essays and practical tips. A good resource for all students."
—*KLIATT*

"Upbeat tone and clear, practical advice."
—*Book News*

"What's even better than all the top-notch tips is that the book is written in a cool, conversational way."
—*College Bound Magazine*

"Invaluable information."
—*Leonard Banks, The Journal Press*

"The Tanabes literally wrote the book on the topic."
—*Bull & Bear Financial Report*

"Experts on the application process."
—*Asbury Park Press*

"Filled with student-tested strategies."
—*Pam Costa, Santa Clara Vision*

"The first book to feature the strategies and stories of real students."
—*New Jersey Spectator Leader*

ACCEPTED!

50 Successful
Business School
Admission Essays

SECOND EDITION

By Gen and Kelly Tanabe

Harvard graduates and award-winning authors of
Get Into Any College, 1001 Ways to Pay for College and
Get Free Cash for College

Accepted! 50 Successful Business School Admission Essays
By Gen S. Tanabe and Kelly Y. Tanabe

Published by SuperCollege, LLC
3286 Oak Court
Belmont, CA 94002
www.supercollege.com

Credits: Cover design by TLC Graphics. Back cover photograph by Alvin Gee (www.alvingee.com).

Trademarks: All brand names, product names and services used in this book are trademarks, registered trademarks or tradenames of their respective holders. SuperCollege is not associated with any college, university, product or vendor.

Disclaimers: The authors and publisher have used their best efforts in preparing this book. It is sold with the understanding that the authors and publisher are not rendering legal or other professional advice. The authors and publisher cannot be held responsible for any loss incurred as a result of specific decisions made by the reader. The authors and publisher make no representations or warranties with respect to the accuracy or completeness of the contents of the book and specifically disclaim any implied warranties or merchantability or fitness for a particular purpose. The accuracy and completeness of the information provided herein and the opinions stated herein are not guaranteed or warranted to produce any particular results. The authors and publisher specifically disclaim any responsibility for any liability, loss or risk, personal or otherwise, which is incurred as a consequence, directly or indirectly, from the use and application of any of the contents of this book.

ISBN   1932662170
ISBN13 9781932662177

Manufactured in the United States of America
10 9 8 7 6 5 4 3 2 1

Gen S. Tanabe, Kelly Y. Tanabe
   Accepted! 50 Successful Business School Admission Essays / Gen S. Tanabe and Kelly Y. Tanabe. --2nd ed.

          p.   cm.
          ISBN 1932662170

          1. College Guides   2. Business School--United States
          3. Reference   I. Title

This book represents the combined knowledge of dozens of students and admission officers who generously gave of their time and insight. We would like to dedicate this book to these people. And to you, our dear reader, we hope you will take the lessons in this book and use them to get into the business school of your dreams.

TABLE OF CONTENTS

The Admission Essay: Your First Marketing Test

Marketing Yourself in Your Essay

Your first business school marketing test will not take place in a classroom. It will be wherever you are when you sit down to do your business school applications. Getting into business school takes a lot more than good grades and GMAT scores. While you have many strengths, so do the eight other applicants who are vying for that single spot on the admit list. How will you make your application rise to the top? How will you convince the admission officers that you are the best candidate for admission?

In most cases you'll do it through your admission essays.

Business school admission essays make a big difference in whether or not you get accepted. Yet, you can be the greatest writer in the world or have years of impressive work experience and still fail to capture the attention of the admission officers in your essays.

Writing a successful business school admission essay is not about being a good writer. Nor is it about cataloging all of your work experience in 500 words. The reality is that writing a successful admission essay is a unique blend of art and science. There are some traits that every successful essay shares. You'll learn what these are by reading the sample essays in this book as well as the interviews with business school admission officers. But each essay is also a unique reflection of the writer. We'll show you how to find an original essay topic that captures and highlights your unique strengths and personality. We'll also share with you the 25 most common essay writing mistakes that you must avoid.

Why are admission essays so important to getting into business school? At their most basic level, admission officers use your essays to understand who you are, why you feel that business school is your next logical step and how you will add value to their campus. While admission officers can surmise whether you can handle the academic rigors of business school by evaluating your grades and GMAT scores and they can get a sense of what other people think about you through recommendations, the essays provide the only way they can judge how your background, talents, experience and personal strengths come together to make you the best candidate for their school.

For you, the admission essays offer the best opportunity to market yourself to the business school. You start with a blank sheet of paper and through careful selection, analysis and writing, you create a picture of yourself to impress the admission officers and make them want you for their school.

How this Book Helps You Write Successful Essays

The entire goal of this book is to help you craft the best essays possible. To do so we will explain what admission officers value in essays and how they fit into the overall admission decision. We will reveal how to best present your strengths and skills in writing. We will also share with you 50 admission essays written by students who have been accepted by the nation's most selective business schools. We hope you will both learn and be inspired by reading these essays.

We recommend that you read this book straight through to best understand the importance of the essays, what admission officers are looking for, how to get started and how others have approached the essay questions. Here is a breakdown of what you'll learn in each chapter:

In **Chapter 2**, you will learn how the admission process works and what happens once your application is submitted to the school. You will see how the essay affects your chances of getting accepted and why admission officers value the essay as one of the most important ways to learn about who you are beyond your grades and GMAT scores.

We have brought together a group of admission officers in a roundtable in **Chapter 3** and **Chapter 5** to discuss what they are seeking at each stage of the admission process. They describe what has worked, and perhaps more importantly, what hasn't worked for students in the past.

In **Chapter 4**, you start the essay writing process by evaluating your strengths and selecting topics. This requires you to start asking yourself some serious questions about your background and your future plans. You'll also learn how to test your topics to see if they are the best subjects to write about.

Chapter 6 provides additional insight into mistakes that you need to avoid when writing your essay. You can learn from previous students' costly errors.

In the following chapters we analyze the essay questions that you will have to answer and let you read the essays of successful applicants. Naturally your essays must be your own, but it is extremely useful to see examples of approaches that have worked before.

Perhaps the most common question that business schools ask is why you want an MBA, which is the subject of **Chapter 7**. You need to have some good reasons why you want to spend the next two years of your life pursuing a business degree and how it fits into your overall career plans.

Once you've established your reasons for choosing to earn an MBA, the next question you'll most likely have to answer is why you want to attend that particular school. In **Chapter 8**, we address how to answer this question since it requires some research beyond the glossy brochures from the business schools.

In **Chapter 9**, you will learn how to tackle questions about what you can bring to an MBA program. You could give a laundry list of your achievements, but on a higher level you can demonstrate how your achievements will help you contribute to the business school's community.

Leadership is a quality that all business schools value. In **Chapter 10**, you will see how you can demonstrate your leadership abilities and your views on leadership in your essays.

Business schools are interested in learning about your achievements and how they relate to your ability to be a successful businessperson. Essays about your most important achievements are covered in **Chapter 11**.

Naturally, business schools realize that not everything goes according to plan, that you have weaknesses as well as strengths or have worked to overcome challenges or obstacles in the past. **Chapter 12** addresses these types of questions, and you will learn how you can use a negative or challenging experience to demonstrate your strengths in difficult times.

Along with leadership and the ability to overcome challenges, teamwork is also an important skill in business, and business schools want to learn about your ability to work with others. In **Chapter 13**, you will read essays that deal with this subject.

Essays Do Make a Difference

"The essays are very important," says Rosemaria Martinelli, director of MBA admissions and financial aid at the Wharton School at the University of Pennsylvania.

While the other pieces of the application are important, the essays hold special significance to admission committees. They allow you an opportunity to make the strongest case for why you should be admitted and can share who you are beyond GMAT scores and GPAs.

"They're one of the few areas for applicants to tell their story and to demonstrate to the committee who they are, what their path is and what their passions are both personal and professional. Everything else is just a data point," she says.

Juan Carlos Loredo places similar importance on the essays at the McCombs School of Business at the University of Texas at Austin. He is a student member of the admission committee, for which first year students read prospective applicants' essays and make recommendations about whether they should be admitted.

He says that if he looks at two students with similar scores and grades, "The difference is made by the essay."

While you certainly have no two days that are the same, by sharing with business schools a typical day, you illustrate how you spend your time and your priorities. In **Chapter 14**, you will find essays about a day in your life.

With the growth of international business, it is increasingly important to have international experience, and cross-cultural experience essays are the subject of **Chapter 15**.

In **Chapter 16**, there are essays about extracurricular activities, something that business schools value because they can demonstrate your leadership skills and ability to interact with others.

Business schools want to see what your priorities are. You can show what's important to you through your most valued possession, the topic of **Chapter 17**, and your passions, the topic of **Chapter 19**.

It is also important for business schools to understand what significant events and people have shaped who you are. In **Chapter 18**, there are essays about defining moments in your life, people you admire and your family.

In **Chapter 20**, you will understand the importance of the optional essay, the essay in which you can choose to write about something that hasn't been addressed elsewhere in your application. This essay question can be one of the most influential of all of the essay questions, and you don't want to miss out.

You'll learn finishing touches in **Chapter 21**, such as how and when to recycle and the important role that editors play in helping you to develop your essays.

Throughout the chapters, you will also find **Stories from Real Life**. These reflect triumphant and at times even tragic experiences through the eyes of admission officers and students alike. While these experiences can be humorous, they are meant to also be insightful and provide guidance.

Your first marketing lesson begins now!

CHAPTER TWO

Executive Summary

The Application

Getting into Business School

It would be nice if all it took to apply to business school was a couple hours filling out applications and then tossing those applications in the mail. The reality is that the process takes months of preparation. Some students spend weeks tweaking their choice of action verbs on their resumes.

So you may be wondering what happens once you submit your application. Who are the people who read your application, and what are they looking for? Do they really scrutinize every word?

Unfortunately, not every business school is the same, and some may have slightly different procedures than what is outlined in this chapter. However, what follows is generally true for most schools. Plus, there are a lot of similarities in the criteria that the various business schools use to judge your applications. Let's begin by looking at all of the pieces that make up your business school application.

Application Overview

There are three basic questions that business schools want to answer before admitting you. Can you handle the academic coursework? How does an MBA fit into your future? And, why do you want to attend this specific institution? Business school admission officers try to find the answers to these questions through what they learn about you in the different parts of the application. Let's take a look at these parts:

Application Form. In the application forms, you will describe your work experience, awards or honors, involvement in activities or public service and basic educational background. This gives the business schools information about your schooling, career history and interests.

Grades. Business schools will evaluate your ability to handle the academic coursework from your undergraduate grades and, if you have earned graduate credits, your graduate school grades. They pay particular attention to courses that measure your quantitative skills such as math, economics or accounting classes.

GMAT. In addition to your grades, business schools also measure your academic readiness from your Graduate Management Admission Test (GMAT) scores. There are three parts to the GMAT: Analytical Writing Assessment (AWA), Quantitative and Verbal. In the AWA section, you will write two essays. AWA scores can be between 0 and 6, with half point intervals.

The Quantitative and Verbal scores are between 0 and 60, although it is rare to receive Quantitative scores less than 7 or more than 50 or Verbal scores less than 9 or more than 44. The Quantitative section has multiple-choice questions on Data Sufficiency and Problem Solving. The Verbal section has multiple-choice questions on Reading Comprehension, Critical Reasoning and Sentence Correction. The scores from the three parts of the GMAT form the total score, which is between 200 and 800. Obviously, higher scores are better.

Admission Essays. Business schools typically ask a series of essay questions. Common questions include why you want to attend business school, why you want to attend their specific school and how your work and leadership experiences make you a worthy candidate for admission. In Chapters 7 to 20, we cover the most common of these essay questions in detail as well as provide examples of essays written by successful applicants. Business schools use essays to understand your motivations for attending business school, to see the fit between you and their school and to get a better picture of who you are beyond your grades and test scores. Many admission officers consider the essays to be the most important part of the application.

Recommendations. In addition to learning what you think about yourself, business schools want to learn how others evaluate you. You will most likely ask managers and professors to write recommendations to describe your preparedness for business school.

Interview. Many schools offer interviews, and some schools require them even if you have to do it by telephone. Since so much of business is composed of verbal communication, these interviews play an important role in the admission process. Business schools use interviews to see how you compare in person to your written application, to see the fit with their school and to gain further insight into how business school fits into your future career plans. They might even throw you a few curve balls to see how you deal with stress.

How Many Schools Do I Apply to?

There are students like Juan Uribe who apply to just one business school, in his case Harvard Business School, and get accepted. For most students, however, one school is not enough. But how many schools should you apply to?

You shouldn't go overboard. Anthony M. Fernandez, another Harvard Business School student, says that when trying to hedge his bet he ended up applying to too many schools.

"It was a waste of time and money, not to mention a waste of the schools' admission resources," Anthony says. He applied to 10 schools.

A good balance between too many and too few is usually between six and eight schools, including one to two each of reach and safety schools.

Even Juan, who was accepted to the single school that he applied to, would probably do it differently the second time around. "I was probably foolish in only focusing on one school. I should have seriously considered other schools," he says.

What Happens Inside the Admission Office

As you drop your application into the mailbox, you may feel like it disappears into a black hole of oblivion. You might imagine that it gets dumped onto a slush pile of other applications, never to be read again. Rest assured, this is not how the process works.

Business school admission officers like to say that the admission process begins long before you start filling out an application form. It starts when you decide to apply to business schools and begin thinking about which school is the best fit for you. Part of the admission staffs' job is to make sure you have all of the information that you need about their schools to make sure their program suits you. They do this by sending out catalogs, creating detailed websites and holding informational sessions throughout the country and even abroad.

Once you've decided to apply to their school, most admission offices have administrative staff who gather all of the application materials

Why You Should Apply Early

Imagine what would happen if the IRS let us choose when to turn in our taxes—we would all wait until the end of eternity to do them. But most business schools have deadlines where you can choose in which round to apply. So you may wonder why you'd ever want to apply in one of the early  rounds instead of letting the natural procrastinator in you take advantage of the later deadline.

In almost all cases you should apply as early as possible. At many schools, the later you apply, the more competitive it can become. In part this is because admission officers can give more time to review applications that are received early. Remember, the vast majority of us are procrastinators. Plus, applying early shows that you are serious about attending a school and that it is one of your first choice selections.

Randall Dean, the former director of admission at Michigan State University, says that each year he noticed that a group of applicants sent in their applications at the latest deadline clearly after having applied to more prestigious programs. This second group of students raised some eyebrows in the admission office. "You can't help but question how motivated these students would be if we're not their first choice," he says.

However, while it is generally to your advantage to apply early, if you aren't ready it is better not to rush. "If you don't think you are putting forth your best effort. If you don't think your essays are solid and you've lined up people who can speak about how you've added value in their recommendations. In other words, if you are just not ready I would want you to wait. I would rather you submit in the second round so that you can use the time to create the best application possible," says Colleen McMullen-Smith, associate director of MBA admissions and career services at Carnegie Mellon University.

So aim to get your applications turned in by the first round. Just don't sacrifice quality to do so.

together and make sure that the packets are complete. In some cases, they re-enter information from applications that are sent by mail instead of through the Internet.

Before making their final decisions, many schools interview applicants. Some interview all students who meet their prescreening requirements even if just by telephone. In some cases, the person who interviews you becomes your personal liaison to the admission office.

When it comes to essays, each is carefully scrutinized by one or more readers. If you're surprised that the business schools read all of the essays received, you'll be even more surprised to learn that they are most often read twice or even three times. Usually initial readers review the application and give recommendations to accept or deny. These initial readers may be admission officers or even second-year MBA students. Then, the director of admission, assistant director or admission officer gives a second reading. In some cases if the first and second readers agree, the decision is made. If not, the application is reviewed by third readers. At other schools, decisions are made in a committee meeting of admission officers that may also include current business school students.

As you return from the post office after mailing your application, you'll probably feel a sense of relief. You've done your part. But for the admission officers at the schools, the work has just begun. By the time the process is over your application will have gone through a thorough review process. Your essays will probably be highlighted and covered with notes written in the margin by several readers. Every scrap of paper that you submit will be looked at and evaluated.

It is only after all this work is completed that final decisions are made and that glorious fat envelope that holds an acceptance letter is mailed to you.

Be a Smart Shopper

"If you're going to buy a $100,000 car, you would never buy it unless you test drove it," says Wenny Tung, a recent graduate of Duke's Fuqua School of Business. In the same way, you should conduct due diligence on prospective business schools. She says the best way to do this is to meet current students and visit schools.

While on campus, ask yourself questions to see how well you'd fit in. Investigate the facilities, observe the students and how they interact and sit in on classes.

"It's important to be a smart shopper. To not make a visit before making a purchase shows a lack of good sense," says Randall Dean, former director of admission at Michigan State University. He says that if you can't visit, you should at least meet with the admission staff when they give presentations on the road.

After all, going to business school is expensive, and so is the process to get in. Saul A. Lopez, a recent graduate of the University of Pennsylvania's Wharton School estimates that he spent $4,000 on the admission process. He spent this on a GMAT review course, GMAT test fees, four application fees, travel expenses to visit all the schools and dinners with his wife so she could "remember who I was," he says. But he doesn't regret his expenses. Saul says, "It's only wasted money if you don't get accepted. Otherwise it's an investment."

Admission Officer Roundtable

How We Decide Who Gets In

Inside the Admission Process

We've brought together a stellar group of admission officers to form a roundtable discussion so you can read in their own words what they are looking for when they decide whom to accept. You'll see that they aren't afraid to let you know what works—and what doesn't.

 Q **What qualities do you look for when selecting students for your school?**

Rosemaria Martinelli

Director of MBA Admissions and Financial Aid
University of Pennsylvania Wharton School

We look at a lot of factors such as their academic horsepower from their undergraduate education and GMAT score, their work experience and their extracurricular involvement. We also look at the quality of their essays, to see if they can articulate past plans and the motivations behind them and if they exhibit a certain level of self-awareness.

For us one thing that is extremely important is academic aptitude/horsepower. You can't get accepted without it. We want someone who has strong academic abilities, with some quantitative experience. We want to know that they've had enough in-depth experience either in school or at work so that they can successfully contribute to the class. We want every student to be an equal and full member of the class team.

We're also looking for applicants who have had some exposure to leadership. They need to possess some of the qualities of a good leader such as confidence and self-awareness. They also must have discipline and yet still be willing to take risks.

Finally, we want to make sure that as potential students in our school they are aware of who they are, where they are and what their plan is. We want them to show us how this all fits together and how their past links to their future. This kind of awareness and the ability to express it in their applications is really critical.

Donald C. Martin

Associate Dean for Enrollment
University of Chicago Graduate School of Business

Given my experience in admissions and having gotten to know my colleagues at other business schools, I have come to believe that we are much more similar than different in terms of what we are looking for in a student. Where we have differences is usually in things like the number of essays we require or how we conduct interviews. But in terms of how we evaluate applicants, we're all looking for similar things.

There are three primary areas that we look at when evaluating an applicant. The first is academic achievement, the second is professional development including work progression and career development and the third is personal qualities including leadership and involvement in extracurricular and civic activities. Each of these three areas is extremely important and equally weighted.

It's common that we see an applicant who is strong in one area such as someone with a terrific academic record but whose personal qualities are less competitive. What we're looking for is a combination of the three areas.

To make our decision we have a process that we feel provides the most thorough and equitable evaluation of each application possible. Every single applicant who submits an application will have his or her application read in its entirety by our admissions committee. No person is cut out because he or she has a bad test score or hasn't worked as long as others. Every applicant is given an equal and fair review by the admissions committee. This has been a hallmark of our admissions process. Students should be pleased to know that if they take the time to complete their application they will have a full review by the committee.

Randall Dean

Former Director of Admission
Michigan State University Broad Graduate School of Management

One important quality that business schools consider is work experience. While at Michigan State, our minimum requirement was two years of full-time work, but the average candidate to our school actually had five years.

When evaluating applicants we want to see both quality and quantity, and experience didn't have to necessarily be business experience. We know that people come from all walks of life. However, we do want the applicant to show us what they have learned from their work experience.

We also take a good look at the applicant's undergraduate performance and GMAT score, which are good predictors of how well they will do in our program. These factors are more important for candidates with less work experience.

I also think it is becoming more and more important to see if the candidates have a good curricular fit. In other words, do they have a good personality fit? For example, we are a very strong school in supply chain management and human resource management. We want to see candidates who have a passion in those areas. If we saw candidates who want to do something very different like real estate, we would question if Michigan State is the right school for them.

The interview really helps us to make sure that the candidates have a good personality fit. It also gives us an opportunity to do some fact checking. Some applicants tend to embellish their experience in the application. The interview gives us a chance to get some in-depth insight into what they have done.

Surprisingly, when I was in admissions, about 30 to 50 percent of applicants did not meet the minimum application requirements. Some candidates had no work experience while others did not meet our minimum criteria for the GMAT. Unless there was some resoundingly unique situation, those candidates would be sent through the process rather quickly.

Colleen McMullen-Smith

Associate Director of MBA Admissions and Career Services
Carnegie Mellon University

We're looking for applicants who not only have strong academics and the aptitude to handle the curriculum but who are also comfortable with the quantitative aspects of our program. In addition, personal qualities are important. We want students who have experience working in collaborative teams and who can show leadership. This is important because we see ourselves as building future business leaders.

One thing we look for is consistency in the application. We see a lot of really high GMAT scores, but we also have to determine if these high scoring applicants are going to work well in a team. Someone can have a high GMAT score, but if I speak with them and they don't have strong communication skills and can't articulate why they want an MBA or how the degree will assist them, there's an imbalance. In fact, they could be the most quantitative students and be able to analyze anything, but if they're not able to effectively communicate, it's all for naught.

Kristina L. Nebel

Director of Admissions and Financial Aid
University of Michigan Business School

The baseline that we are looking for is someone who can thrive in an intellectually challenging environment. We measure this through their past courseload, grades and GMAT scores. This year the average GMAT score for our admitted students was around 700. It always amazes me how high the scores are. That's one aspect of what we are looking for, but it only tells part of the story.

Through their applications we want to get a sense of the applicants' leadership potential and their ability to create results—what they've been doing, how they have made an impact on their organization, can they handle ambiguity, are they are willing to take risks? We want to know if they work well in teams and if they are able to take initiative.

Another important question we ask of each applicant is this: Do you understand what Michigan is about? We are known for our approach and commitment to action-based learning and the ability for students to build on our broad-based curriculum utilizing the many offerings of the Business School and the rest of the University to create a robust and customized experience. We expect students to understand this, be excited by it and be able to communicate how they are going to approach their Michigan MBA experience to achieve their objectives.

We also look to see if they understand the broader role of business in the community and society, if they understand that they will contribute not just in their career but also outside of their jobs. Business is a powerful force of social change—we understand that, and we expect our students and alums to hold that belief as well. We want to know if they are the kind of person who will be involved both inside and outside of the classroom. Will they take a leadership role to add to the community here at Michigan and beyond?

Successful applicants should be able to articulate why they want an MBA and what they hope to get from the degree. In this sense, there needs to be a thread of continuity. Where have they been? Where do they want to go? How will Michigan help them get there? If they haven't gone through that thought process of what they want to achieve during their MBA experience and beyond, they may not be successful in getting admitted.

Julie R. Barefoot

Assistant Dean and Director of MBA Admissions
Emory University Goizueta Business School

First, we look for academic preparedness and potential. Our goal is to admit candidates with strong analytical skills who can handle the rigorous coursework of the program as well as add value to MBA class discussions. The specific academic background of the applicant doesn't really matter. In fact, most students in our program do not have backgrounds in business—we enroll individuals from a wide variety of academic and work disciplines. However, whatever the undergraduate (or graduate) school major, the applicant must demonstrate through prior coursework and/or the GMAT results that they are analytically prepared for MBA studies. If they haven't had specific business coursework, we look for proxies such as statistics, economics or math courses. We also look specifically at the GMAT quantitative score as a good measure of their current quantitative preparation.

The second major component in our review process is assessing the quality of a candidate's work experience. It's difficult to explain what it is that constitutes "strong pre-MBA work experience" primarily because we're not looking for one particular job or one particular company on an applicant's resume. In fact, we welcome candidates who bring a diversity of work experience to our program. However, we are looking to see if the applicant can demonstrate (through their essays, interviews and recommendation letters) that they have added value to their company or organization. Have they taken on additional responsibility? Have they been recognized by supervisors and colleagues for their motivation and leadership? We are clearly looking for leadership potential in all of our candidates. We also want to admit and enroll students who have been involved in their communities and organizations because that is an excellent indicator that this candidate will be involved and be a contributor at Goizueta. This involvement can be through a number of means—for example, student government or sports or Habitat for Humanity or fraternal organizations; we want students who are committed to leading and being an active part of our community.

 What common mistakes do students make when choosing people to write recommendations?

Randall Dean

Former Director of Admission
Michigan State University Broad Graduate School of Management

Letters of recommendation are very important and I really want to read a professional recommendation from someone with whom you have worked in the past. Academic recommendations from a professor are nice but don't really help me to gauge professional aptitude. The MBA program is in essence a work environment. Recommendations should demonstrate readiness for the program, and they are even more important if you've had a weaker academic background.

You want to pick your recommenders very carefully. It was surprising to me how many times we would get a recommendation that wasn't very strong or even complimentary. That would be a major red flag for an application. If your recommenders rated you as an "average" employee that could really hurt your candidacy.

Another risky strategy when it comes to recommendations is when you try to find a person with high name recognition to write your recommendation. Often, this person does not know you well enough to write a personal recommendation. I would suggest that you find someone who—regardless of whether or not they are well known—is familiar with you and will write positive things about you and your accomplishments.

Julie R. Barefoot

Assistant Dean and Director of MBA Admissions
Emory University Goizueta Business School

The most common mistake is that candidates select a recommender who is well known, famous or has an impressive title, but doesn't really know them in any meaningful way. My advice to applicants is to ask individuals who know you well and can make substantive comments about your ability to contribute to MBA class discussions and to be a valuable employee after you graduate.

 What might students be surprised to learn about the admission process?

Randall Dean

Former Director of Admission
Michigan State University Broad Graduate School of Management

If applicants do their homework, then they shouldn't be surprised at how the process works. Most programs make public the information on the typical candidate who

Interview Mistakes

When Colleen McMullen-Smith, associate director of MBA admissions and career services at Carnegie Mellon University, interviewed one student, she noticed that he had a really high GMAT score and decent essays. She had some pretty high expectations but was let down.

"All this candidate could say was my father had an MBA, my brother had an MBA and I have a 720 GMAT score. I was trying to learn more about what he wanted to do, but it seemed that he wasn't able to tell me more of his story," she says.

Interviews allow business schools to attach a face and personality to your application. They are your opportunity to demonstrate that you have the skills crucial for success in business, which include the ability to express yourself and your ideas through verbal communication.

About this candidate, McMullen-Smith says, "Also being a career counselor, I asked myself if I put this person in front of a recruiter, are they going to be able to articulate to that recruiter why this particular company is a good fit for them, or will they just say that they are smart?"

In addition to communicating effectively, you also need to act professionally. As a student admissions fellow at the Fuqua School of Business at Duke, Wenny Tung interviewed prospective students. She has interviewed applicants who haven't dressed professionally, chewed gum and even used foul language during interviews.

She says, "If you're supposed to be representing my school, how are you going to represent yourself to a recruiter? We make them comfortable, but sometimes there's a certain line crossed of being too comfortable."

gains admission and what their program's strengths are. Most of us make ourselves available for interviews with applicants. I don't think admission officers are trying to surprise students or purposely knock them out of the process. We all have a strong incentive to put together the best class that we can. The reality is that every admission officer is feverishly looking for the best candidates to admit.

Colleen McMullen-Smith

Associate Director of MBA Admissions and Career Services
Carnegie Mellon University

> Students would be surprised to learn that we are not expecting them to have their entire career path mapped out. It's not something that's required to being a strong candidate. It's okay to say that the MBA is going to allow you to evaluate where your skills will be best used.

Kristina L. Nebel

Director of Admissions and Financial Aid
University of Michigan Business School

> Contrary to what students may imagine, we don't create this big stack of all the management consultants and pick the top 10 out of the pile. It's a case-by-case assessment. There isn't a compartmentalization of all the consultants or all the investment bankers, for example. We compare everyone to everyone. Students get so worried about how they are going to differentiate themselves. What's important is that you describe how you got where you are and the experiences you've had. Those experiences are naturally unique.

> We also have students with strengths that range across the board. We have folks who have come from Wall Street but also those from public service. The classroom thrives on the fact that you may be sitting next to a guy who studied economics, a woman who studied English literature and a past Peace Corps member. It all adds to the flavor in the classroom and is a critical part of the entire MBA experience.

Rosemaria Martinelli

Director of MBA Admissions and Financial Aid
University of Pennsylvania Wharton School

> Students are most surprised when they meet us on the road and find out how unpretentious we are and how fun loving we can be. We're not the buttoned down, all-business types that they imagine. This is really a reflection of our community. We work hard and we play hard. We've had some students

say that they were just blown away by how warm and open everyone from the admissions office is, which was the complete opposite of what they expected.

 What advice do you have for students applying to business school?

Randall Dean

Former Director of Admission
Michigan State University Broad Graduate School of Management

A lot of students ask, "Should I make a visit for an interview?" I strongly recommend that they take advantage of making a personal visit. To make it a mandatory requirement, of course, isn't realistic. But if someone from Japan or Brazil made the effort to visit our school that made an indelible impression on the admissions committee. If you're a domestic student, there's almost no excuse not to make the visit. It gives you the best chance to make a good impression.

Colleen McMullen-Smith

Associate Director of MBA Admissions and Career Services
Carnegie Mellon University

One of my soapbox issues is the importance of preparation. I think it's critical that students do extensive research and visit the school to go beyond the normal information sessions. When visiting the school they should observe what takes place and look at the interactions between students. If the students are cordial and collegial and they're smiling, that's a good thing. If you're not getting a good feeling, it's a sign that the school may not be a good fit. Picking the right school goes beyond the academic characteristics. You want to be in an environment that is also conducive to your learning.

I'm always shocked when I see applicants who have taken the GMAT in October and are not happy with their score. Preparation should begin nine to 12 months before the first deadline. If you take the GMAT nine months before applying, you would still have time to take it again and make the first deadline. Letters of recommendation should be done very early too. I encourage you to sit down with the people who will write your recommendations. Let them read your essays to get a sense of where you're going. Make sure they're clear on how you have added value in the workplace. Recommendations for business school are very different from those for getting a job. You want to make sure your recommenders have enough time to write a strong recommendation.

Julie R. Barefoot

Assistant Dean and Director of MBA Admissions
Emory University Goizueta Business School

If there is anything about your background that you feel deserves an explanation, then you should take the time to explain it. Don't leave it up to the admission officer to fill in the gaps. Candidates often make this mistake in regard to their academic record and gaps in their work experience. They think that admission officers won't notice the poor grades or the gaps, but we do. Of course, we understand what is going

---

Will Gimmicks Give You an Edge?

So you think you can beat the system by sweetening up the admission officers with a basket of homemade cookies or a witty tchotchke? Admission officers have received everything from homemade sweets to boxing gloves to "fight" their way into the school. But does it work?

"I don't advocate it. That's not going to help your case," says Kristina L. Nebel, director of admissions and financial aid at the University of Michigan Business School.

The reality is that these kinds of gimmicks don't work because they don't tell the admission officers anything about your ability to handle the coursework, your business acumen or how business school fits into your career plans. You're better off spending the time honing your application and perfecting your essays.

on in the economy, and we don't believe that there is any shame in having multiple jobs or a gap in work experience. Having said that, a candidate does need to explain the gaps. The same is true with weak grades. An MBA experience at a selective program is academically rigorous and demanding; it is critically important that the applicant explain to the admissions committee the reason for their poor grades and what will be different about the applicant's MBA academic experience. I don't recommend a lengthy essay, and I certainly would not advise making excuses, but please do tell us what happened in the past. The applicant should make sure the admissions committee has a complete and accurate picture of their academic and work history.

Donald C. Martin

Associate Dean for Enrollment
University of Chicago Graduate School of Business

Follow directions. We're not trying to play games with you, and we're not trying to psyche you out. We have reasons for the questions that we ask. Please don't assume that you know something different than what we're asking.

Timeliness is also important. Try to apply earlier rather than later. If you're really thinking about this, the sooner you apply, the sooner you'll hear an answer. But don't sacrifice the quality of the application for the speed in which you can submit it. If you're approaching the November deadline and you haven't had the chance to have someone look over your application, wait until the next deadline. Timeliness is important but you should not be so hasty that you send in something that is not your best work.

And, finally, don't approach this process as if it's a life or death situation. If you don't get in, maybe there's a new door that opens for you. I encourage applicants to relax and be diligent but don't be so diligent that you can't sleep. It's not worth it.

The Essay Writing Workshop

Essay Writing Workshop

Nobody said it was going to be easy to think of the greatest achievement that you've had in the past 20- or 30-something years of your life. It's even more of a challenge when you have to encapsulate it in a few hundred words.

But that's exactly what business schools are asking you to do—and not just for your greatest achievement but also why you want to attend business school, why their school is the best fit for you and what you have to offer your fellow b-school students.

It's no wonder then that many students are a nervous wreck when it comes time to put pen to paper or fingers to keyboard and write their admission essays. But before you even begin writing you need to do some thinking. A successful business school essay is not only well-written but it also conveys insightful thoughts and relevant examples from your experiences. It shows your ability to analyze your past, present and future as well as express how an MBA fits into your overall life goals. Your essays reveal the research that you have done about the school and highlights the motivation behind your decision to apply. So before you can write you need to think.

Let's begin by sifting through your life experiences to figure out which topics will fly and which ones will flop.

Finding the Perfect Topic

Before you start brainstorming what to write about, it's important to know what questions you will be asked. The best way to do this is to look at the applications of the schools that you are applying to and make a list of their questions. One of the most common complaints from admission officers is that applicants do not answer their questions in the essay. Don't fall into this trap. Tape the list of questions above your computer, on your bathroom mirror or inside your refrigerator to remind you of what you need to answer.

In general, you'll find that most questions fall into one of three major categories:

- Why do you want to attend business school?
- Why did you choose this particular institution?
- What value will you add to this school?

The wording may differ among schools, but the bottom line is that admission officers want to understand your reasons for attending business school, how you think you will fit into their institution and what special skills and talents you bring to the class.

Besides these three major questions, business schools may also ask more specific questions. To learn about your business acumen, they may ask you about your most important achievement or greatest challenge. To understand your priorities, they may ask you to describe a day in your life. To get a sense of your interpersonal skills, they may ask about your extracurricular activities or to write about a time when you had to work in a team.

As you begin to brainstorm topics, it's critical that you ignore what you think the business schools want to hear. Another major complaint from admission officers is that students try to give what they think the admission officers want to read. (Be sure to read the *Admission Office Roundtable* in the next chapter since they will tell you exactly what they are looking for in your essays.) If you try to filter your ideas by what you assume will impress the business schools you'll severely limit your chances of coming up with a winning topic that is both original and a true reflection of you.

Brainstorming a Topic Begins with You

Moms were always good at asking those impossible to answer questions. Remember when yours would ask you, "What do you want to do with the rest of your life?" Or how about the time she asked if the person you were dating was "the one?" These difficult to answer, highly personal questions that mothers are famous for asking are very similar to the types of questions you'll find on your business school applications.

The questions business schools ask require you to search deep into your heart and soul and really ask yourself some honest, introspective questions. So, if your mom hasn't done so already, now is the time to ask yourself these serious questions about what you've done that you are proud of, why you want an MBA and how the degree fits into your future plans. Fortunately, the answers to these questions will form the basis of your admission essays.

Grab a sheet of paper and start scribbling some answers to the following Mom-inspired questions:

- What made you decide to attend business school?
- What have you done at work or in other activities that you feel has prepared you for business school?
- How have you demonstrated leadership?
- How have you shown management ability?
- When and how do you work as part of a team?
- How have you excelled in your work?
- What tangible contributions have you made as an employee?
- How have you shown initiative?
- What is your biggest workplace success? Failure?
- What qualities are most important to you in selecting a business school?
- What do you hope to learn in business school?
- How will you apply this knowledge to your future career plans?
- Why is it essential for you to get an MBA? Why pursue it at this point in your life?
- How will you enhance the community of business school students at the school?
- What makes you unique?
- What do you like to do outside of work? Why?
- Who is the most influential person in your life? What have you learned?
- What is the most difficult thing you have done? Why did you do it?
- What was the best and worst experience you've had at work and in your personal life?

By answering these types of questions, you will be able to generate a list of your most meaningful influences, experiences and beliefs. This list will provide all of the examples and themes that you will use when answering the various essay questions.

Keep Asking Why

You could really cheat yourself out of a great essay when answering the above questions if you simply write down the obvious. If you answered the question about the most difficult thing that you have done by simply writing, "Climbing to the top of Mt. Kilimanjaro," you're only halfway done. You need to ask "why." Why did you climb it? (Hopefully, not just because it was there.) Harness and use the full strength of your analytical ability. Remember, business schools want students who can analyze problems and issues. Apply this analysis to your essay topics. The truth is that your essay is also a demonstration of your ability to analyze as much as it is a test of your ability to communicate.

Don't just accept your first response either. Keep pushing yourself by asking "why." Here is the thought process that should happen inside your head. Don't forget to take copious notes on your answers.

QUESTION: What is the most difficult thing you've done?

ANSWER: Climb Mt. Kilimanjaro.

QUESTION: Why did you climb it?

ANSWER: I enjoy challenges.

QUESTION: Why specifically did you choose to challenge yourself in this way?

ANSWER: I wanted to see if I would fail. I have a fear of failure and felt that if I were able to successfully make it to the summit I might have more self-confidence in other areas of my life.

Now you're getting somewhere and beginning to uncover some significant and also interesting thoughts about yourself. But don't stop now! Keep pushing deeper until you can go no further.

Why did you choose a physical challenge such as mountain climbing instead of a mental challenge? Now that you've summited Kilimanjaro have you actually seen an improvement in your self-confidence? See how you keep asking questions about your answers to uncover deeper and more interesting thoughts and analysis?

You need to be this rigorous for every topic idea. It's not easy and will take days—even weeks—to complete. But if you outline your topics in this manner you will discover some truly unique aspects about yourself that will form the basis for answering all the essay questions.

Eliminating Bad Topics

If you've taken the time to subject yourself to the intense brainstorming and self-reflection described above, you should have several pages of potential topics. Not all of these are going to be winners. To help you narrow down your list you need to see how each potential topic or idea will contribute to the overall message of your essay and application.

Through your application—and especially in your essays—you are creating a picture of yourself for the admission officers. Generally, you

Like a Fine Wine, Let Your Applications Age over Time

Saul A. Lopez thought it made perfect sense to submit his applications as early as possible, with a goal to meet each school's second round deadline. With only a month to the second round deadline at one of his top-choice schools, he completed that application first. He was "pleasantly surprised" with a rejection letter.

He explains, "By the time you fill out later applications you will know what you want to emphasize about yourself and enough people will have read and provided you feedback on your essays." Luckily, he was accepted by the Wharton School, his other top choice, an application he completed later in the process due to their (then) rolling admission process.

Anthony M. Fernandez had a similar experience. "Looking back, I feel that the essays for my last application were far better than the ones for my first application," says the Harvard Business School student.

want to convey to the business schools that you are prepared for the academic rigors, that you have a plan for using your education and that you will be a leader who contributes to the class and the business community at large.

For each experience or idea that you have listed, think about the greater message it conveys. Struggling with a learning disability as a child may be an early example of your tenacity, which you also show at work. Being able to work in a foreign country and deal with business practices that are different from your own may reveal how adaptable you can be.

Not all the messages you convey need to be personal characteristics. Some may explain how you have come to realize something important. Your work as a management consultant may have motivated you to get an MBA to further your career because you realized that you have reached your limits without more education. Your volunteer experience as a sailing instructor may reveal a passion for being on the water, which will also influence your future career choices.

Next to each topic idea, write down the larger message that it conveys. It may be an example of a character trait, an important realization or simply something that gives you pleasure. Try to analyze each to uncover what messages you can draw out of it. A good essay is not just a well-written narrative. A good essay is an analysis and demonstrates your analytical ability.

You will discover that some ideas don't have a strong message or that they convey something that you don't necessarily want to share with an admission officer. Now is the time to cross out these ideas. Keep only those that will help you make your point. This means you may have to axe a great, funny story that just doesn't contribute to your overall message. Do it. Nothing ruins an essay faster than reading a paragraph that–no matter how interesting–contributes nothing to the rest of the essay.

While doing this exercise be sure to refer back to your list of specific questions from the business school. It should be taped to your bathroom mirror, remember? If your topics or ideas don't address the specific questions of the school, they should also be eliminated.

Once you have your list of topics, the message that they convey and which questions they can answer, it's time to share. It will save you a lot of time and effort if you get some feedback before you start to write.

Share Your Ideas with a Friend

There's a reason why there is a thriving industry built around therapy. It actually helps to talk things through. This is especially true for essay writing. If you are stuck on a topic, not sure if it's a good one or just want to make sure you've thought of everything, talk it out with a friend, family member or colleague.

Ask these people if it sounds like an interesting topic and if it conveys an important part of your background or personality. You will be surprised by how much discussing your ideas with someone—even before you've written a single word—can help.

If you share your ideas with more than one person, you may get conflicting responses. That's fine. At this stage you just want to dissect the topic and get feedback. Often this feedback will help you explore the potential of the topic, uncover new possibilities, alert you to possible problems and fine-tune your message.

So share your list of topics with anyone who will listen. Keep an open mind and listen to what they have to say. It will only help you to write a stronger essay.

Aim to Be Unique

One of the most important traits of a good essay is that—like a snowflake—it should be one-of-a-kind. You don't want to write an essay that someone else could also write. This is hard to do since every applicant is answering the same questions. Plus, if you come from a popular business field such as consulting or investment banking, your business experience may be similar to hundreds of other applicants from the same profession. Even when it comes to outside activities, a lot of business school applicants share a love of such things as travel, outdoor activities like snowboarding and even a desire to push themselves through extreme sports like triathlons and rock climbing.

So with all of these potential similarities, how do you write an essay that is different? It goes back to your ability to analyze your experiences and to be self-reflective about what you have learned. Like the classic Kurosawa movie, *Rashomon*, where various witnesses describe the same crime, each interprets the same event differently. Let's look at an example.

For Good or Bad News, Use the Optional Essay

In addition to essays about why you want to attend business school or what your future career plans are, you may also be asked if there is anything else that you would like the admissions committee to know. This is the optional essay question. While technically this essay is optional, many admission officers view it as very important. Some even read this essay before any other essay.

"I read the optional essay first. It sets a frame for me before I move into the other parts. It gives me what has gone on in this person's life," says Colleen McMullen-Smith, associate director of MBA admissions and career services at Carnegie Mellon University.

You can use the optional essay to write about something important to you that doesn't fit in elsewhere in your application. The optional essay can enhance your strengths to the business schools.

"The biggest mistake is not using that optional essay to your advantage, not using the optional essay to speak about what makes you unique. It's really important to address the things that you couldn't address elsewhere," says McMullen-Smith.

However, don't use the optional essay to just write more for the admissions committee to read. "It really should add value and address something that you feel you haven't been able to express elsewhere," says Kristina L. Nebel, director of admissions and financial aid at the University of Michigan Business School. "We read a lot of essays, and adding another into the mix unnecessarily doesn't help your case. Use judgment in deciding to write it or not."

The optional essay can also be the place to explain a less than perfect record. Admission officers will see lower undergraduate GPAs or gaps in your employment, and it is better to explain the circumstances in the optional essay rather than ignore them.

"I'd rather you tell us what's going on than have the admission committee fill in the holes by guessing," says Nebel.

Imagine that you are an avid rock climber. If you've carefully analyzed and reflected on why you enjoy climbing and what motivates you to scale a barren cliff every weekend, you will find that the reasons are as unique to you as your personality. Now you will probably have some shared reasons with other rock climbers. Since these are not unique, you can safely eliminate them from your list. While there is nothing wrong with acknowledging some of the more common themes, such as the joy of finding a route to the top of a sheer rock face, it should not be the central theme of your essay.

A lot of applicants will submit essays that are not unique simply because they did not take the time to analyze beyond the obvious. If you write an essay where the theme is that "perseverance can overcome any obstacle" or "education is the key to success" you stand a very real chance of having your essay passed over because it sounds like hundreds of others.

Use the Thumb Test

One of the best ways to determine if your essay is original is to use the "thumb test." It's easy to do and highly effective. When you have a rough draft of your essay or even a detailed outline, read it over completely and then take your thumb and cover your name at the top. If you can imagine putting someone else's name at the top of the essay (such as a college buddy or co-worker) and the essay would still work, then you might not have an original essay. However, if only your name can be at the top then your essay passes the "thumb test" and it is original.

You can do the same thing with your list of topics. Ask yourself, "If I write about this will I be the only one who can write this essay in this way?" If the answer is "no," then you may need to rethink your approach.

Ultimately, you want your essays to be unique and original. But the good news is that if you analyze your topic deeply enough and you are genuine in your answers, it will be unique. It's when you don't push yourself far enough in your analysis or when you try to second-guess what the admission officers want to hear that you get into problems with originality.

Everyone has a snowflake-like essay inside of them. You just need to work to discover it.

Take the Passion Test

Now that you have a shorter list of topics that you've thought about, shared with some friends and tested for originality, the last test you should apply is passion. One of the best ways to get inspired when creating your essays is to choose a subject that inspires you. When you write about something that you are passionate about, the words will flow more fluidly and contain energy that the reader can actually feel jumping off the page.

The passion test is especially useful when you face the common dilemma of choosing between a topic that you think the business schools will be impressed by and a topic that you are truly passionate about. For example, on a question about what you do in your spare time you might be tempted to write about how you play the stock market instead of your true love of macramé. You might think that stocks and bonds will be more impressive to a business school admission officer than weaving cords and beads into plant hangers. But if you're passionate about macramé and don't take any pleasure in investing, your essay about investing is likely to appear uninspired and generic. But your essay on the delight you get from matching the right macramé fibers and beads to create the perfect plant hanger would be filled with passion and would be much more interesting and memorable.

Admission officers have a sixth sense for detecting when you are catering to what you think you should write rather than being true to yourself. So if you have topics on your list that you are not passionate about, put a big "X" next to them. Focus on those ideas that excite you and that truly represent who you are. These will become the best essays because they come from the heart.

Time to Write

Think you have a winning topic? Now the only thing left to do is to write. So pull out that notebook or fire up the laptop and start putting words to the page. The ultimate test of whether or not your topic is a good one is to actually turn it into an essay.

Admission Officer Roundtable

What Makes a Successful Essay

What Makes an Essay Successful

Now that you are ready to write it is important that you know what admission officers think about essays. It's doubly important that you also know what they are looking for when they are reading your essays. After reading this roundtable you'll have a new appreciation for the importance of your essays and an understanding of how they will help you get into business school.

 How important is the essay in the business school admission process?

Julie R. Barefoot

Assistant Dean and Director of MBA Admissions
Emory University Goizueta Business School

They are very important to us in the context of your application file. You do not have to necessarily hit a homerun on every essay, but if you do not present solid, strong communication skills in your essays, you will not be offered admission. The bottom line is that the essays can make or break a candidate, and they can make a huge difference in scholarships. We use the admissions application to determine who is awarded scholarships, and we provide scholarships to as many as half of our class. The awards range from one-fifth to full-tuition awards. So, in the sense of scholarships, the essays are doubly important.

Randall Dean

Former Director of Admission
Michigan State University Broad Graduate School of Management

The essays are a very important part of the application. The essays along with the interview are the two key pieces that help with assessing the candidates' writing and communication abilities. The best candidates have the ability not only to do quantitative analysis but also to advocate and share information in their essays and interviews.

Colleen McMullen-Smith

Associate Director of MBA Admissions and Career Services
Carnegie Mellon University

The essays are very, very important. A resume is just a snapshot. The essays give us an insight into a particular candidate and what has brought them to seek an MBA. If you look at the other pieces of the application, although they're important, those that are more narrative—such as letters of recommendation and the essays—tell us a lot. A GMAT score or GPA can be a fairly limited indicator. There are many people who are bad test takers but who are very smart.

Kristina L. Nebel

Director of Admissions and Financial Aid
University of Michigan Business School

The essays are very important. The essays give applicants the best opportunity to tell their story. The interview also adds some insight into the person, but when you think about how we learn the most about them, it really comes from the essays. It wouldn't be a stretch to say that the essays are the life of the application. Be sure to tell us your story in a natural and honest way—be yourself.

Donald C. Martin

Associate Dean for Enrollment
University of Chicago Graduate School of Business

The essays are extremely important. This is one of the opportunities that applicants have for us to get to know them better and for them to express themselves in their own unique style. The essays often help to corroborate other impressions that we're getting from applicants' work history and their conversations with our staff. They're an integral part in helping us understand an applicant's career progression and in evaluating their personal qualities. We value the information in an essay and read every one of them thoroughly.

Q What are the qualities of a good business school admission essay?

Colleen McMullen-Smith

Associate Director of MBA Admissions and Career Services
Carnegie Mellon University

Good essays are really tailored to the particular school. It's much easier for students to do general essays and fill in the blank with the school's name. Believe it or not at least once a year we get a student who forgets to change the school's name.

Telling their story is important. From time to time, I get an essay that says, "I want an MBA, to be a manager and to go from junior marketing assistant to director of marketing." That's okay, but what I'd really like to know is what has the applicant learned as a marketing assistant? I also want to know how an MBA from our school will help them achieve their goal of becoming a director of marketing. In particular I want to know what it is about our school that makes them feel we are the best fit for their goals.

You can automatically tell when an applicant is writing what they think we want to know instead of what they honestly feel. They'll write something like, "You're the only school that does quantitative analysis." Of course, we know that's not true. It's as if they think such statements are going to make us feel warm and fuzzy. But we don't want to read about something only because the applicant thinks it's what we want to hear. We're not geniuses but we're pretty smart. Just be genuine.

Rosemaria Martinelli

Director of MBA Admissions and Financial Aid
University of Pennsylvania Wharton School

Communicating honestly and having self-awareness is important. It is better to explain motivations or lessons learned rather than just describe accomplishments. We like to see a generosity of spirit, a willingness to contribute and intellectual curiosity. How have you taken advantage of opportunities? What have you done in your current position in life? What were those critical transition points that helped you develop into who you are today? It's these intangibles that we find most interesting in an essay.

Donald C. Martin

Associate Dean for Enrollment
University of Chicago Graduate School of Business

We want candidates to answer the questions that we ask and not go off on tangents. If we ask why you would like to attend the GSB, we'd like to know the answer. There's a specific reason why we ask that question.

In any essay we want to see applicants as they see themselves. We want applicants to try to be who they are and not over-inflate their accomplishments.

We also appreciate it when applicants follow directions by staying within the word limit. With three or four essay questions times several thousand applicants, that's a large number of essays we're reading. When we ask for 500 words and someone gives us 1,500 words, that's a negative indication for us. We don't read beyond the estimated word limit.

Kristina L. Nebel

Director of Admissions and Financial Aid
University of Michigan Business School

As simplistic as it sounds, the first quality of a good essay is that you answer the question. For candidates applying to more than one school, you need to be careful about reusing essays. It's easy to think that the first essay of one school is similar to the third essay of another school to which you're applying. But unless the questions are actually identical, the answer will be slightly off. When reading an essay it is easy to spot where an applicant has missed the question.

Julie R. Barefoot

Assistant Dean and Director of MBA Admissions
Emory University Goizueta Business School

The applicant should take the time to prepare and submit well-written essays that answer the questions asked in the application. The applicant's responses should be conveyed in a clear writing style, free of typos and grammatical errors. In addition, the applicant should give specific examples in their background (work and life experiences) to support their essay responses. For example, every business school has distinct questions, but almost every school asks you to recount a significant accomplishment and also to tell us why you want to obtain an MBA. We're not naïve. We know that candidates are cutting and pasting essays to use for multiple schools, and that's okay. Nevertheless, the applicant needs to make sure that they have addressed the specific question at hand. We want to read essays where the candidate has articulated how they have added value to their organization and how their experiences will contribute to MBA class discussions.

Through Goizueta's essay questions, we give applicants the opportunity to show their personality and their interpersonal skills because those elements are also very important for long-term career success. We try to give every applicant a chance to shine, but applicants need to spend time and prepare well-written essays that will give the admissions committee a clear and positive picture of their ability to contribute to our community and classroom.

Candidates also need to remember that an MBA program is an analytical experience. It's more than just developing marketing or advertising ideas. An MBA program experience involves conducting cost and benefit analysis and developing complex business strategies. Therefore, we look for strategic thinking skills in the essays beyond just the style and substance. We want to have insight into the applicant's thought processes.

 What common mistakes do students often make on the essay?

Kristina L. Nebel

Director of Admissions and Financial Aid
University of Michigan Business School

As good as spell check is, we sometimes read why XYZ school is a good fit for them and it's not Michigan. Don't try to cut and paste these things.

On our essay about goals, a common mistake is that applicants won't tie their goal into why they want an MBA. For example, they will say why they want to study finance, but they won't describe how Michigan's curriculum and offerings will help them do this. They don't describe what they hope to gain from a Michigan education.

Sometimes the essays can be very generic. You need to do something beyond looking at the viewbook and website and spitting back the words that we wrote. Talk to students and alums so you can personalize why the program is good for you. Anyone can say, "I'm really interested in marketing and I'm interested in Michigan because it's a good school for marketing." But it's better to say, "In talking to students X and Y and faculty member Z…" You need to not only show us that you are interested in studying marketing but also that you really understand our program beyond the glossy brochures.

Randall Dean

Former Director of Admission
Michigan State University Broad Graduate School of Management

We had a very strict requirement that essays should be no longer than one page. You'd be surprised at how many applicants completely ignored that requirement. When things got busy, we'd read the first page and that would be it. Some applicants sent in four to five pages. What a waste since we simply didn't have time to read past the first page.

One of our reasons for such a strict requirement was that we were actually trying to assess how well applicants follow instructions. Either they didn't pay attention or they were aware of the limit but decided they deserved special attention. Sometimes we would get booklets, 20- to 30-page manifestos. They think they might stand out as unique but typically they would stand out as the first to go into the garbage can.

Julie R. Barefoot

Assistant Dean and Director of MBA Admissions
Emory University Goizueta Business School

If candidates don't answer the question, it tells us that they don't follow directions very well, and this can hurt them. We've had essays that have clearly shown that candidates are not a good fit for our program because their examples are incomplete or off the mark. We've even had an applicant write about a significant accomplishment that wasn't their own accomplishment! Another common mistake is not giving clear examples in response to the question. In addition, many applicants do not proofread their essays, or they demonstrate a weak writing style. Applicants need to take the time to proofread and have others proofread their essays for both grammar and style. Additionally, review your essays for content and clarity.

Admission is not just determined by the GMAT and GPA. Candidates must have strong essays and convey a passion that fits with their career plans. If the story about their post-MBA plan doesn't make sense, that concerns us. A candidate with a liberal arts background who worked in advertising may write that he or she wants to be a strategy consultant. This could make perfect sense, but it's up to the candidate to show us how and/or why they are a good fit for that career path. There has to be support for their plans.

Colleen McMullen-Smith

Associate Director of MBA Admissions and Career Services
Carnegie Mellon University

> Sometimes applicants do not use good judgment. Every year I read two or three essays where the applicants' experiences may be accurate or true, but the language or examples were not appropriate. On our question on ethics, we've had applicants write about how on a business trip they had to decide whether or not to cheat on their spouse. That may be an ethical decision, however it's not appropriate in terms of a business school essay. You need to keep it professional. Not every ethical dilemma is an appropriate topic to write about.

 What might students be surprised to learn about what you are looking for in essays?

Colleen McMullen-Smith

Associate Director of MBA Admissions and Career Services
Carnegie Mellon University

> A student asked, "Do you really read the essays? Surely you can't read them all." The answer is "yes," we actually read them all. Sometimes we even follow up with questions to the applicant about what we read in an essay. When we do, the student is shocked. The essays tell us a lot and we read them in detail. We highlight significant sentences. We put notes in the margins. We really do read every word that you write.

Rosemaria Martinelli

Director of MBA Admissions and Financial Aid
University of Pennsylvania Wharton School

> So many applicants try to present what they think the admissions officer wants to hear rather than being themselves. A lot of people give us data points, but they don't give us the take-aways. You should be honest about your experiences, not exaggerating in order to impress the admissions committee.

Some applicants just try to impress so much that they make their experiences sound like so much more than they were.

It's also amazing how many people forget to answer the questions. They get into being creative but in doing so they miss answering the basic questions. Those judgment calls can hurt an application much more than anyone can possibly imagine. Judgment is also a part of leadership. We're not looking for literary writers. We're looking for business writers.

When applicants forget to tell me about the value of their experiences, I wonder why working at a Burger King or at a consulting firm makes sense for them. It's important that you explain the significance or value of what you have done. Ask yourself why. A leader is constantly checking where they are, what they're learning and how what they are doing is affecting them. Why are you a fast tracker? What did you learn? How did that help you decide what you did next? You need to constantly provide us with context and analysis.

Donald C. Martin

Associate Dean for Enrollment
University of Chicago Graduate School of Business

This is such a wonderful, renowned institution, but in some students' essays there is an overabundance of compliments. They try to write about all the things that are great about the school, citing the Nobel Prize winners, describing this as an almost perfect institution and declaring that they couldn't see themselves anywhere else. No place is perfect. If someone sounds overly complimentary, that is not something that we find to be very useful or impressive.

We also don't find that being arrogant helps. It's one thing to put your best foot forward, but the manner in which you do so is very important. If someone tries to say that we would be at a dreadful loss if we didn't have them at the school, that is not helpful. Some applicants think that the way you make yourself stand out is to sound as if you're larger than life. I think that's bad advice. You make yourself stand out by being yourself. We aren't looking for clones or for superheroes. Confidence is great; arrogance is not. We're looking for real people.

 What advice do you have for students writing their admission essays?

Randall Dean

Former Director of Admission
Michigan State University Broad Graduate School of Management

Do your homework on the program. This might be more relevant for international students, but we received so many essays where it was plainly obvious that the candidate had not done their research.

You also want to take advantage of the opportunity given by the essay. The nice thing about the essay is that it's not a timed affair. For the GMAT essay you only have a certain amount of time. With admission essays, you have the opportunity to do a nice job. We look at style, content, grammar, spelling and the ability to communicate in a proper manner. We received several essays every year with significant misspellings, poor uses of grammar and even some with other schools' names in the essay. For most admissions people, that's the kiss of death. Just relying on the spell check is not enough. If you're going to take the time and effort to go through this process, I recommend you find someone to read your essays before you send them to us.

Rosemaria Martinelli

Director of MBA Admissions and Financial Aid
University of Pennsylvania Wharton School

One of the most important things is to do your own personal self-assessment. Begin to outline the critical turning points and even the failures in your life. Then identify the messages you want us to learn about you. Plot in where you can use some of those things even before you start writing. Think both personally and professionally because we want to know both. Think about where you can include those parts of yourself, those unique things that make you who you are.

Once you start writing you can be pulled completely off track. So start early. I would start months before your essays are due. Ideally, start your self-assessment over the summer months and by September start outlining what you want to do. Whether you apply in round one or round two, this will give you plenty of time to write and edit and then re-write and re-edit.

Also, you should not write your first choice school's application first. You should write those after you've had some practice. As you apply to more schools, you will figure it out. That's part of the discovery process.

Julie R. Barefoot

Assistant Dean and Director of MBA Admissions
Emory University Goizueta Business School

If you want to give yourself an added edge, make sure you know the school(s) to which you are applying. Some candidates start working on the essays before they really know the school. Applicants need to put their best foot forward. Where it's appropriate, let the admissions committee know that you have researched the school. How do you do this? Don't just insert the school's name in a sentence. We can tell when candidates really know Goizueta–our curriculum structure, the strength of our community, etc.; this knowledge can give a candidate the added edge. Finally, be sure and proofread your essays for typos and make sure that if you mention the school by name that you have the correct school with the correct essay–more candidates than you can imagine insert the wrong school name when they cut and paste their essays–admissions officers notice these errors right away!

Q What are some essay topics that just don't work no matter how hard you try?

Kristina L. Nebel

Director of Admissions and Financial Aid
University of Michigan Business School

In prior years, we had a question about a setback or failure. This gives us various insights into someone's ability to overcome obstacles. Inevitably you'll get someone telling about how they didn't make the high school football team. People sometimes didn't think about the impact of this question. We're not interested in something that happened that long ago or that is insignificant in contrast to a more recent setback. With this essay I also have seen people cross the line, telling us about how they lost the love of their life. While I want to learn about you as a person, you need to use judgment in choosing your topics.

As we read a file and are making notes on it, sometimes we'll come to an essay and it seems very "I" focused. As you look at that essay, you literally see a lot of "I"s on the page. "I" did this, "I" did that. We want people who can lead and make things happen, but most people recognize that you're not going to do this solo. The essay can be a little individualistic both from content and visually. The flip side is someone can write what their team accomplished, but not about the role they played on the team. Both extremes are a mistake. You need to find a balance between these two extremes.

Finally, when asked to cite an accomplishment, we sometimes have applicants noting the fact that they got promoted or passed the CPA exam. On the first topic, the promotion itself doesn't tell me as much. I would rather hear about what you did that led to the promotion. On the CPA issue, while a wonderful achievement, I can see that you are a CPA from your resume. Writing an essay on it does not add that much value.

SIX

The 25 Most Common Essay Writing Mistakes

Avoid Common Essay Writing Mistakes

Before you read examples of real essays we want to share with you the top 25 most common essay writing mistakes. These are mistakes that students commit every year and that have a disastrous effect on their chances of getting admitted to business school. Learn from their mistakes so you don't commit any of these errors in your own essays.

1.

NOT ANSWERING THE QUESTION. It may seem like an obvious mistake, but many applicants don't answer the question. Or they answer part of the question but not all of it. If you are asked about a time that you've been a leader and the impact that your leadership had, don't just describe when you have been a leader. Make sure that you also address the impact of your leadership. This is a mistake that many students make when recycling their essays or using the same essay for one school for another. If you do recycle your essays, edit them carefully to make sure that they completely answer the question asked.

2.

SHOWING THAT YOU KNOW NOTHING ABOUT THE SCHOOL. Business schools take pride in the fact that they each have their own strengths. They want to see you address those strengths and how you will benefit from them. While it can be tempting to copy and paste your essays from one school to another, you'll want to make sure that each essay addresses the strengths of each school. Admission officers can tell when your essays are so general that you have used them to apply to multiple schools or haven't done your homework about the strengths of their program. In at least one of your essays, be sure you show how the school's particular strengths match your needs.

3.

PARROTING BACK WHAT'S ON THE WEBSITE OR BRO-CHURE. To try to show their knowledge about a particular business school, some applicants go to the school's website or brochure and copy text from them into their essays. Admission officers are oftentimes the ones who write this material and it does not impress them to see their own descriptions of their schools in essays. You need to do your own research. Visiting a school and talking to some of its students and faculty is critical. By doing so you can include in your essays what you have learned from sitting in on classes, interacting with students or observing an activity. This kind of insight demonstrates that you have taken the time to research the school and understand what it has to offer you.

4.

ASSUMING THE PERSONA YOU THINK THE SCHOOL WANTS. Some applicants try to be who they think the admission officers want them to be. They may say that they want to go into a field that they are not excited about, exaggerate strengths that they think will impress the school or even try to flatter the admission officers by declaring that their school is the only one for them. Unless you mean it, the admission officers will see through hyperboles such as these. It is better to reveal your honest intentions, strengths and opinions. You will produce more genuine and believable essays that will ultimately help you get admitted.

5.

NOT REVEALING ENOUGH ABOUT YOURSELF. The questions you answer may be about your family, a figure you'd like to have dinner with or international travel you've done. But the bottom line is that the admission officers ask these questions as a way to learn about you. So instead of writing an autobiography of a historical figure or a detailed travelogue of the places you've been, make sure the focus is still on you. If you want to use a historical figure in your essay, you might write about what you would plan to learn from him or her and why this is important to you. If you approach your essay from a travel standpoint, you would want to spend time on how it has affected you versus your daily itinerary. In other words, regardless of the question remember that the essay is still about you.

6.

TRYING TO BE FUNNY WHEN YOU'RE NOT. It takes a very skilled writer to write a humorous essay. If you're not this type of writer, your business school essay is not the place to try to be witty. You can't miraculously change your writing style overnight. Often your attempt at humor may appear trite or just plain silly. It's better to stick to your own style.

7.

GOING OVERBOARD WITH CREATIVITY. The business school essay is not a creative writing project. While creativity is not necessarily a bad thing, you should not make it the focus of your writing style. The business school essay is really business writing, which is more focused on content and ideas rather than delivery. Don't sacrifice the clarity and content of your essay in order to make it creative.

8.

FAILING TO SEE YOUR ESSAYS AS PART OF THE LARGER PICTURE. You can think of each of your essays as a chapter in a single book. While each is important, it's also important how the chapters go together to form the book. In other words, think about the overall impression that your essays convey. Do they provide a consistent picture of your accomplishments and goals? While essays do not need to be closely tied to each other, they should not be so divergent or contradictory that the admission officer is confused about who you really are. Write your essays with the understanding that they will be read together along with the rest of your application.

9.

NOT KNOWING WHY YOU WANT TO GO TO BUSINESS SCHOOL. As you answer the essay questions, you will need to explain why you want to earn an MBA and how you plan to use the degree to advance your career. The more you understand your motivations for earning the degree, the stronger your essays will be. This is something that you need to think about and try to tie into at least one of your essays. You don't need to have every step of your future career worked out because admission officers understand that a business school degree will help you figure this out. But you do need to have some good reasons about why you want an MBA at this point in your life.

10.

NOT SHOWING A CONTINUUM FROM PAST TO PRESENT. In your essays, admission officers are looking for your story. They want to see the past and present as well as a glimpse of the future. From your past, you should explain what you have studied or learned from your employment to prepare you for a business school education. From the present, you should describe why you want an MBA. For the future, you should give some hint at how you intend to apply your degree in your career plans. These questions do not have to be answered in one essay. In fact, you will probably choose to address each in a separate essay. However, you should make sure that after reading all of your essays you get a sense of each of these three important parts of your life. If you are missing any of these parts, there will be a hole in your story.

11.

FORGETTING TO TIE IN YOUR GOALS WITH THE SCHOOL. It's important that you not only explain your career goals but also elaborate on how the business school will help you to achieve these goals. Admission officers want to see a connection between their school and how it will help you meet your personal and career goals. This helps them to see what you will gain from attending their school.

12.

NOT WRITING ABOUT INDIVIDUAL ACHIEVEMENTS. While it's important to show that you can be a team player, it is also important to define your individual accomplishments. Some students only write about their accomplishments as a part of a team but never address what they contributed as an individual. This is a big mistake. If you are writing about a group accomplishment, make sure to describe how you individually contributed to the success of the group.

13.

WRITING A RESUME IN PARAGRAPH FORM. Your essays should be more than glorified resumes. In other words, don't just list your accomplishments. Describe the importance of them and what you have gained from the experiences. Analyze and reflect on their value. Whether you have been a management consultant or a chef, you need to explain how your work experience fits into your path to an MBA and how you hope to apply your experience in the future.

14.

FAILING TO USE GOOD JUDGMENT. Your biggest setback in life may have been when you didn't get chosen as the lead in a high school drama production or when you were unfaithful in a relationship, but these are not the kind of setbacks that business schools need or care to know about. Ask yourself if what you are writing is an appropriate subject for a business school essay.

15.

NOT EXPLAINING WHAT YOU HAVE LEARNED. More important than your actual accomplishments is what you have gained from them. This is the key piece of information that admission officers want to know. As you're writing your essays, think about what you have gotten out of the experience, how you would approach a similar situation differently and how you have applied your knowledge to other interactions.

16.

RUNNING OUT OF TIME. It is a mistake to think that you can develop meaningful essays overnight. Thoughtful essays take time. Thinking about your goals, the meaning of an MBA and your life's accomplishments takes a lot of quality time. Give yourself enough time to think about what you've done and what you believe in to develop the strongest essays possible.

17.

NOT TAKING ADVANTAGE OF THE OPTIONAL ESSAY. For a lot of business schools, the last question they ask is whether you have anything else that you'd like the admission officers to know about you. In most cases, you should take advantage of this essay question. You can use it to highlight a strength that you haven't highlighted elsewhere or you can use it to explain a blemish in your academic or professional record. This is the first essay that some admission officers read when looking at the essays because they believe that this open-ended question is where you can really describe what is important to you and what makes you unique. There are no guidelines for what you need to write about so you are free to write about whatever is meaningful to you that you want the business school to know about. Take advantage of this opportunity.

18.

NOT ADDRESSING AN OBVIOUS WEAKNESS. You might think that if you have less than perfect grades or if you were unemployed for a period of time it's best to hide it. This is a mistake. Admission officers will see your transcript and the dates of your employment. It is better for you to offer an explanation for these weaknesses than for them to wonder what happened and assume the worst. Remember that you should provide an explanation, not an excuse.

19.

NOT HAVING A POINT. As you are writing your essays, it's not enough for the essays to be well written and tell a good story. They also need to convey the message that you want the admission officers to know. In other words, what strengths do they reveal? How do they portray you? What impression do they leave? Try to take a step back to examine the message that you are sharing with the reader through your essay. If you can't find it then your essay is probably lacking in focus.

20.

WEAK INTROSPECTION OR ANALYSIS. Admission officers don't just want to know about your actions. They want to get inside your head to understand your thoughts and motivations. Try to share what you are thinking to give them a better idea of who you are. Admission officers expect to see both self-reflection and analysis in your essays.

21.

SKIMPING ON EDITORS. It's difficult to edit your own essays when you are so close to the material. One of the best ways to improve your work is by having someone else give you feedback. Find business school students or graduates, friends and family members who are strong writers to look at your work. Ask them to point out weaknesses, to check for continuity and to make suggestions on how to strengthen your messages. Their feedback is a necessity to writing a successful essay.

22.

LOSING YOUR VOICE THROUGH THE EDITING PROCESS. While it is critical that you get feedback from editors, it is equally important that you use the feedback as a guideline for your writing but that you still retain your own voice. You don't want your work so heavily edited that it no longer sounds like you. Similarly, if you blindly accept everyone's suggestions you might end up with an essay written by committee rather than by you. Editing should enhance your writing not take the place of it.

23.

NOT PROOFREADING. Almost every admission officer can point to an essay each year in which an applicant writes the wrong school's name. A little proofreading can go a long way. It's not enough to use your computer's spell check. Take the time to read each word of your essays and check grammar, punctuation and spelling. Or if you aren't skilled in copyediting, find someone who is.

24.

EXCEEDING THE WORD LIMIT. When the business schools ask you for a 500-word essay, you don't want to give them a five-page paper. Yet, that is what some students do every year. While admission officers are not going to count every word that you have on the page, they do give word limits for a reason. They have hundreds of essays to read and if each applicant includes a couple hundred extra words that can result in many hours of extra time. If you don't want to be penalized for not following directions or, worse yet, have an admission officer stop reading in the middle of your essay, stick to the word limit.

25.

NOT TAKING SOME TIME AWAY FROM YOUR WRITING. Like a fine Napa wine, essays take time to develop. Often the best way to improve your essays is to take a break from writing them. So write your essays and then allow yourself some time away. When you return to look at them you'll have a fresh perspective and will be able to see how you can improve them.

These are the most common essay writing mistakes. Keep these in mind as you write your own masterpiece. Simply by avoiding these mistakes you can save yourself a lot of unnecessary aggravation and you will ensure that you have the strongest essay possible.

ESSAYS

Why Do You Want an MBA?

NOT SURPRISINGLY, THE MOST COMMON ESSAY question is about why you want an MBA. Business schools want to understand how you have prepared for the degree, what you hope to attain from it and how it fits into your long-term career plans. You need to show a continuum of where you've been, where you are and where you would like to be. It is also vital that they understand why an MBA is critical to your success at this point in time in your life.

As you think about how to answer this question, consider the three phases of your life. First, think about previous experiences.

- How have they prepared you for business school?
- How have they made you come to the conclusion that you would like to pursue an MBA?

Then think about your current state.

- What makes now the best time for you to earn an MBA?
- What knowledge and skills do you hope to obtain from the degree?

Finally, think about your future plans.

- What are your future career goals?
- How will an MBA help you achieve your career goals?

As you are writing about this continuum, be as specific as possible. It is more powerful to describe specific skills you have gained from work or how you have developed management or leadership skills than to just give a job description. Ultimately, you want to create a story of why you want an MBA that makes sense from your past, present and future.

multidisciplinary
actively
influence

I am con

highly
compatible

united

Essays: Why Do You Want An MBA?

Patrick J. McGinnis
Wharton School at the University of Pennsylvania

My desire to study at the Lauder Institute and the Wharton School of Business represents a natural extension of my educational and professional pursuits over the last seven years. I chose a path that allowed me to develop a strong background in foreign affairs and international business. I am now prepared to enter a multidisciplinary graduate program that will encompass and synthesize these two disciplines while preparing me for a career as a venture capital investor in Latin America. Considering my experiences at Georgetown University and JPMorgan Partners, I am convinced that the Lauder Program is highly compatible with my intellectual and professional goals.

When I entered the School of Foreign Service at Georgetown University, I longed to develop a global perspective. I grew up in a small town in Maine and had never traveled beyond the eastern seaboard. At Georgetown, I studied with diverse and talented peers and faculty from around the world. I chose to focus on International Economics and the emerging trade relations between the United States and Latin America. As I deepened my knowledge in these areas, I contributed my own perspective to the academic dialogue on trade. I wrote a paper entitled "NAFTA: Devaluation and Disillusionment" that was published in Hemispheres, an international affairs journal at Tufts University. My senior thesis explored the evolution of foreign direct investment regimes in the regional trading blocs of the Americas. In parallel, I developed a specialization in Latin American studies and spent a year in Argentina as a Rotary Ambassadorial Scholar.

Upon graduation, I sought to combine my interest in trade with a regional emphasis on Latin America. In the Latin America group at Chase Securities, I developed solid corporate finance skills and gained exposure to the most prominent companies in the region. Over time, however, I realized that my team could not fundamentally influence the operations of our clients. As our client roster was heavily weighted toward established businesses, I realized that I wanted to actively influence the operations of earlier stage businesses. I pursued this interest when I joined the Latin America group at Chase Capital Partners (now JPMorgan Partners) four years ago. When I was invited to join CCP, I was extremely pleased since the group had expressed a preference to hire a native of Latin America. I believe I was successful in the interview process due to my knowledge of the region, my language skills and a strong cultural fit with my new colleagues.

As an Associate at JPMorgan Partners Latin America, I collaborate with entrepreneurs, managers and colleagues to redefine the business landscape in the region. By working alongside management teams to address the financial and operational needs of companies that are in different stages of maturity, I identify opportunities and take action to support their development. Whether I'm working from São Paulo, Buenos Aires or New York, I invest in and monitor companies throughout the region and seek to provide resources that will create leading businesses and lasting value. I find my work incredibly rewarding because I believe that investing in emerging companies brings positive change to Latin America. My team frequently backs management teams that introduce transformational technology and improve infrastructure. These companies provide services that enrich the lives of their users and enfranchise new segments of society. Over the past two years, I have witnessed the ability of technology such as the Internet to democratize access to information and challenge entrenched social and economic structures.

At JPMorgan Partners, I have developed a passion for enabling companies to traverse the uncertain terrain that lies at the confluence of international business, politics and culture. These experiences have inspired me to ultimately lead a team of venture capital investors focused on Latin America. As an investor, I will be able to empower a new generation of business leaders in Latin America and effect change that transcends the realm of business to transform society as a whole. I believe that the Lauder Institute and the Wharton School will help me to develop the teamwork, business and management skills that will make me a more effective investor.

I am attracted to the Lauder Program because its outstanding curriculum assimilates and reconciles my international relations and international business experience. In the Lauder Program, I will embark on a course of study designed to unite and deepen my understanding of the two fields that ignite my interest. Through MBA studies at Wharton, I will explore the underpinnings of the financial and operational issues that have challenged me as an investor. Examining these issues together with my peers will strengthen my capacity to assess challenges from varied perspectives. Further, I will hone the multinational management skills that I have learned from the managers that I most respect in the JPMP portfolio of companies.

I also believe that the Lauder Program will increase the breadth of my exposure to Latin America. I share the program's philosophy regarding the necessity of linguistic and cultural immersion. In the program, I plan to focus my studies on Brazil, a country that represents the convergence of the vast opportunity and the structural challenges that characterize modern Latin America. Over the last two years, I have progressively deepened my knowledge of Brazil. I recently spent two months working in JPMorgan Partners' São Paulo office, and the experience only strengthened my personal and professional interest in Brazil. I view the time I will spend in Brazil as a singular opportunity to heighten my understanding of the country's culture, language and business environment.

Finally, I would like to attend the Lauder Program at Wharton in order to contribute to and learn from a community comprised of faculty and students who are leaders in their communities, families and careers. I have valued my time at the School of Foreign Service and at JPMorgan Partners because both unite people who combine a global point of view with a desire to truly impact their surroundings. I know that I will find such people in the Lauder program, in my learning group, among my professors and throughout Wharton. Within this context, I look forward to learning from my peers and to contributing my own perspective to a community that develops leaders with global vision.

Lyle B. Fogarty
Goizueta Business School at Emory University

Before the advent of strip malls, sprawling suburbs and endless freeways, America had cities. There was activity and diversity within city limits, where commercial and residential uses were intertwined, resulting in continuous interaction with neighbors and fellow citizens. Since the exodus to suburban life and the community center shifting from Main Street to the suburban mall, cities have become, in the words of one urban planner, "cities with billions of citizens and no residents." As population density and diversity decreased, local businesses and urban communities dispersed as well. In the past two decades, metropolitan areas have increasingly recognized the need to concentrate resources on the urban renewal of dilapidated areas. Until about a decade ago, "renewal" was the process of razing distressed areas with new development. More recently, the focus of urban renewal has shifted to redeveloping historic and underutilized structures in an effort to stimulate diverse community centers, such as museums, restaurants, shops and apartments. The resurgence of our cities depends on this creative use of our architecture, history and existing infrastructure.

Getting from Point A to Point B

When Leticia Pearman wrote her essay about why she wanted an MBA, she described where she was, where she was going and where she wanted to be. In other words, she showed the path that she had taken from consulting to strengthening her marketing skills in business school to her future goal of running her own business.

"The essay needs to have a logical progression, how you want to get from point A to point B," says Leticia, a student at Northwestern's Kellogg School of Management.

This kind of progression helps admission committees understand why the degree is important to you and how it fits into your overall plans. There need to be relationships between your past and future, and admission officers need to understand your motivations.

Another student, Peter Gasca, says that when describing your reasons for wanting an MBA, you need to not only show this kind of link but also have both short-term and long-term goals.

"It is especially important to avoid answers that imply you are returning to school because the job market is poor, because you were just dismissed from your last position or you have nothing better to do with your time," says Peter, a student at the Mc-Donough School of Business at Georgetown. Giving solid reasons for attending business school will strengthen your application.

Still, business schools are willing to give you some leeway in your plans for the future. Admission officers understand that you may not have your future mapped out with total certainty.

"Some people say they are going to use this time for exploration. An MBA is a transitional degree. It will allow you to develop a set of skills that will help you in the future. Your time at business school can be a time to explore a future that is not written in stone," says Colleen McMullen-Smith, associate director of MBA admissions and career services at Carnegie Mellon University.

I would like to focus my career efforts on this growing urban redevelopment initiative. There is growing support for these initiatives among city officials and residents, yet these opportunities require business leaders to bring them to fruition. Since my graduation from the University of Notre Dame with a double major in Finance and Spanish, I have developed certain skills that will help me enter and succeed in this arena. For example, at SunTrust Bank, I applied financial analysis techniques to assess the growth potential of bank customers as well as their ability to service the different levels of debt. Several transactions, which I underwrote, pertained to real estate properties and piqued my interest in development. Likewise, as a process risk consultant at Arthur Andersen I have had the opportunity to assess business processes for a variety of clients, analyzing process flows for efficiency, effectiveness, and control breakdowns, as well as implementing continuous improvement methodologies. These acquired skills will strengthen my ability to succeed in future entrepreneurial ventures and are particularly well suited to engage the private sector with urban renewal.

However, there are certain pieces missing before I believe I will truly be ready to realize this vision. In the short term, I see myself rounding out my skill set with an MBA and subsequent work experience. Over the long term, my career goal is to dedicate my time and efforts to revitalizing urban areas. Specifically, prior to entering the urban redevelopment industry, I hope to first accomplish the following objectives:

A Goizueta MBA will assist me in obtaining skills needed to become a successful entrepreneur and effective manager. While in the program I would like to focus on a concentration in entrepreneurship. A concentration in this area will not only help me run my own firm in the future but also help me understand the plights and challenges of small businesses which serve as the building blocks of urban growth and renewal. To complement this entrepreneurial training, I will take elective real estate classes.

During and after the MBA program, I hope to gain some practical field experience with a development group that specializes in these types of urban renewal projects. There are certain peculiarities that successful redevelopment groups master, including forming strategic partnerships with investors and local governments and assessing the potential uses and economic viability of underutilized properties. Building my skills with a successful redevelopment firm will allow me to reach out to more communities in need of these renewal efforts. Not coincidentally, Atlanta is a city that has suffered its share of growth pains and has sought to address these issues in a number of ways. Atlanta Underground is but one example of how joint public-private efforts combined to revitalize an historic urban landmark.

Certain attributes I possess will help me realize this personal goal and more importantly, assist in building communities. In my leadership roles, I have shown an ability to build consensus, an essential attribute when dealing with government officials and affected communities. Trust has always been the foundation of my personal and professional relationships. In many instances, when the project path was not as smooth as anticipated, it was that established trust which allowed my team to shift focus on the go. Finally, community development requires a leader with passion and commitment to the cause, unafraid to make decisions and willing to pursue the vision with all available resources.

Too often businesses focus solely on the bottom line, ignoring collateral effects. In the case of urban renewal, there are not only material rewards to be made, but valuable contributions to the community as well. The architecture is preserved; small businesses emerge and thrive; the sense of community is regained; cities are humanized. It is precisely this combination of a sound business venture with the satisfaction of improving quality of life, which I seek in a future career.

José Chan
Simon Graduate School of Business Administration at the University of Rochester

Combined with my professional experience, an MBA will provide me with the vital academic training in business management crucial to my future success, as a unit head in the apparel division of Louis Vuitton Moet Hennessy (L.V.M.H.), the world's leading luxury products group. In my experience, there is a shortage of highly qualified managers within the luxury products industry, and I am committed to help fill that gap. In addition, my completion of an MBA program will increase the ranks of capable Latino business leaders in the international arena.

Eleven years of combined part-time and full-time professional experience in the fast-paced and competitive apparel industry have provided me with rich and diverse experiences that have helped me grow and mature as a creative manager. I have worked in the wholesale and retail sectors of the industry, with companies in Europe, Asia and the Americas. These experiences made me sensitive to the cultural and corporate subtleties that are woven into the fabric of the modern apparel business. At Nautica, I mastered the art of clear and precise communication through daily correspondence with agents from Brazil, Canada, China, India and Turkey. Then, I took my communication skills to the next level by learning Italian and French and achieving proficiency in both. This helped me triumphantly manage many international situations when working at Countess Mara and while running my own consulting business.

Exposure to international, entrepreneurial small and medium-sized enterprises has also taught me how to function as a team leader. At Sulka I nurtured a small dynamic team that was successful because it logically faced and innovatively analyzed issues without losing focus. I set up logical systems and cross-trained my team to ensure they would be challenged and motivated to grow professionally. My career as an apparel designer has allowed me to fuse my creative abilities with executive acumen in order to become a successful creative manager. More recently, I have used this managerial fusion to serve my community as a bilingual mathematics teacher in the South Bronx.

Customizing Your Essays

Almost all admission officers can recall receiving an essay with the wrong school's name in it. This is perhaps the surest sign that a student recycled the essay, sending the same one to multiple schools and forgetting to change the name.

While admission officers are realistic—they understand that you may recycle some of your material—they don't want you to recycle all of it. In fact, the best essays are tailored to a particular school.

"You really can't use one general essay and plug it into each school. Focusing on each school really goes a long way in your essays," says Remberto Del Real, a student at the University of Michigan Business School. He made sure that his essays were directed at each of the individual schools he applied to.

According to Randall Dean, the former director of admission at Michigan State University, this is the right approach. The admission committee could tell when applicants wrote one general essay and sent it to many schools or when they focused on writing about their program specifically.

"There are many people who apply to 10 or 20 programs and see where they get into. They don't take the time to answer the questions as deeply as they can. It's likely that they are just rehashing the text," he says. While this can help you apply to more schools, it does not help you get accepted by more schools.

Though I have gained much valuable industry experience, I have not acquired all the necessary quantitative and analytical skills to be an exceptional leader in the luxury goods industry. An MBA will give me practical knowledge in functional areas such as finance, accounting, marketing and strategy that I cannot gain on the job. Just as invaluable are the perspectives that I will gain from fellow classmates and professors, who come from different professional backgrounds and nations. Moreover, I expect to establish enduring relationships that will enhance my personal growth, enhance my knowledge of business and inspire me to reach my potential.

In the short-term, the skills and exposure that I acquire will allow me to lead an apparel division of L.V.M.H. In the long-term, I will use my skills to create a model apparel brand and to train the next generation of well-rounded industry leaders. My talents will be used not only for business, but to serve my surrounding community as well.

Juan Carlos Loredo
Jones Graduate School of Management at Rice University

As my University of Texas transcript reveals, I earned a Bachelor of Arts in Theater and Dance. As part of that training, I spent the summer seven years ago working as an apprentice carpenter at the Colorado Shakespeare Festival. That experience more than any other convinced me that I needed to shift career paths. While I truly enjoyed the theater realm, I needed to be challenged intellectually to a greater degree and to have an opportunity for more earning potential. Business administration struck me as a viable possibility and so, once back on campus in the fall, I started exploring that option by taking a few courses in the area. The classes I took proved stimulating and challenging and gave me a strong positive sense of career direction and purpose. I also began to realize that I would need an MBA to improve my chances of moving ahead in the world of business.

My experiences in landscape construction began six years ago with my summer employment at Clean Cut, Inc., a commercial landscaping company. This job enabled me to learn about the issues that are found in an industry with heavy ties to labor. I learned lessons in personnel management that I would utilize later as overseer of a team of workers. Subsequently, when I was hired on full-time, as a management trainee, I found myself learning still more about management and ways of enhancing profits. Four years ago, a larger and more diverse company, Service

Master, Inc., acquired Clean Cut and renamed it TruGreen LandCare. In this larger and more complex corporate milieu I could only watch as better educated and experienced individuals set goals and made plans for the new company. I wanted to be part of that process, but knew that before that could happen, my own business knowledge had to be both broadened and deepened.

The work experience I gained with TruGreen, as well as my own thinking about what I desire in life, helped me refine and solidify my long-term personal and career goals. As regards the latter, I hope to ultimately achieve an upper-management position in a Fortune 500 company or one showing promise of achieving that lofty status. I feel that an MBA is the best way to realize that dream.

To reach my goal, I need more knowledge to draw upon when making business decisions. Although my professional experience has taught me much about the industry in which I currently work, I realize my need for a greater depth of information about other industries and business practices. Through reading about the Jones Graduate program as well as speaking with one of its current students, I have learned about the emphasis that the program places on teamwork. I see no better way of learning than working through real life issues with other students and studying the results of the actions taken.

I am convinced that now is the best time for me to pursue an MBA. I say that for the following reasons: While I have gained much needed work experience at TruGreen LandCare, I feel that my advancement opportunities within the company would be limited without a graduate degree. In addition, I believe that I now have the undergraduate knowledge base, experience, discipline and desire to benefit the most from graduate education.

Lisa C. Olmos
Jones Graduate School of Management at Rice University

While a student at Baylor College of Medicine, Lisa was also admitted to Rice's Jones Graduate School of Management with this essay.

As the daughter of two physicians, I grew up not just aware of medicine but entirely immersed in it. My parents share an office in our home in Washington, DC, built as a residential addition in 1949 by my grandfather, a family physician. I have wonderful childhood memories of answering telephones and filing charts in the office, talking to patients and doing my homework after school in the waiting room. Today, together with one technician and one secretary, my parents continue to successfully manage their own private practices.

I do not expect my own medical career to be similarly structured. In fact, my parents' situation is an extremely unusual one today. With the rapidly changing environment of health care, physicians need to be aware not only of the advances in medical knowledge, but of the economic forces that dictate their ability to implement those advances. Medical technology is improving by leaps and bounds so that expensive machines and instruments are required for physicians in outpatient practice to provide the current standard of care. Our modern hospitals have a tremendous capacity to deliver life support and intensive care, but finance frequently becomes a deciding factor. Drug companies, too, with their tremendous financial clout, are an important element of our healthcare system, providing free samples for indigent patients and financially stimulating research to find new and better medicines, yet charging expensive fees for their products. However, it is the creation of managed care that has truly forced the medical community to face the financial complexities of the healthcare system.

Yet all too frequently physicians leave the practical aspects of the economics of care to others. Many now find themselves in a situation in which insurance company employees, often non-physicians, dictate the extent of care that can be reimbursed, in an attempt to control increasing healthcare costs. This can lead to poor, inefficient patient care and hard feelings all around. In my medical school experience thus far I have witnessed frustrating, though likely well-intentioned, insurance policies in action. At the predominantly Hispanic family clinic in which I worked, a woman visited because of a frightening numbness and weakness in her legs. She needed to see a neurologist. However, we discovered that her employer had switched her to a new insurance plan, and our clinic was no longer an eligible site for her to receive primary care or referrals. Despite the change, she stayed on with our clinic's doctor because he spoke Spanish. She now faced a difficult decision: wait weeks to get another appointment with a new doctor, an official referral and an appointment with the neurologist; or visit the local emergency department.

Our country's health care system continues to be excellent, but we face new challenges in our ability to deliver and reimburse care for everyone. Only with intelligent planning and use of resources can we maintain and improve that quality of care while controlling costs. I believe that physicians who remain dedicated to their profession and to their patients should be the individuals responsible for guiding the economic transition of our healthcare system into the future. I am pursuing an MBA degree because I seek the training necessary to intelligently tackle the obstacles to good, cost-effective health care that have arisen today. Perhaps I will found and run my own medical clinic; perhaps I will be instrumental in financially guiding the hospital or academic program with which I am affiliated; perhaps I will even be a lawmaker or lobbyist who helps institute a new national healthcare system. I do not know precisely what my future holds in store, but I do feel certain that with a strong background in business, management and finance, I will be well prepared to positively influence our healthcare system regardless of my professional sphere.

Camilo Román Cepeda
Wharton School at the University of Pennsylvania

On my wardrobe stands a red Japanese dharma doll with only one eye colored in, reminding me of work in progress, a vision still unfolding. Three years ago, a Japanese friend of mine gave me the owl-faced idol as a gift just before I returned to Michigan from a six-month assignment in Japan. Her only instructions were to fill in one of the eyes after making a wish; coloring the second eye would signal that my dream was fulfilled. When I landed in Detroit and unpacked, I signed the covenant with the dharma, resolute that I would return to the Far East and challenge myself to pursue a career in international business.

Motivation behind the promise recorded on the dharma is based on my desire to continue learning from challenging missions, to apply my work globally and to participate in an exciting environment of vast change and growth. I thrive in environments where entrepreneurial mindsets combined with cross-cultural skills make the difference. Each of these same factors has led me to where I am today and has pushed me to exploit opportunities presented along the way.

Entrepreneurial Allure

Six years ago in February, with an engineering degree under my belt and a dream job as a vehicle engineer with Ford Motor Company awaiting me in Dearborn, I temporarily served as a consultant at Datasage (a friend's software start-up) just to pass the time in Boston until the summer. My position at Datasage challenged me to think as a mini-CEO, directly responsible for contributing to the growth and future health of the company. Within seven months, the company had tripled in employees and venture funding; soon, I too was given an offer to get company equity as a full-time employee. Despite the tempting offer, I made the difficult choice not to stay. Although I would miss the flat organization and the relatively large impact of my contribution, I yearned to work on automotive design in a company with global operations. The CFO of Datasage and my M.I.T. colleagues pressured me to forget Ford; they rationalized I would see limited career opportunity in a 300,000-employee behemoth. Nonetheless, resolved to pursue my dream at Ford, I made it a personal challenge to generate the opportunities I sought.

Engineering in the Global Arena

When I joined Ford, I did not look back ruefully on what could have been at Datasage. Instead, within the first week of meeting my mentor and peer college graduates, I identified the opening I sought - a joint-partnership between Ford and Mazda. I parlayed my previous M.I.T.-Japan intern experience as an engineer at Horiba into a strong assignment in Hiroshima on the first ever Ford-Mazda joint engineering vehicle program. This unique chance not only built upon my cross-cultural team skills, it validated my decision to pursue a career at Ford.

Future prospects: Catalyst of Global Business Development

Melding the entrepreneurial experiences at Datasage with my cross-cultural team efforts as a product engineer, I feel well prepared to develop business relationships beyond the borders of the United States. Augmenting my business acumen with an MBA focused on global management, I believe I can catalyze international partnerships that will yield great growth potential. I target East Asia as the venue of opportunity not only because it is aligned with my extensive experience studying and working in Japan, but also because I anticipate that the tremendous economic growth occurring in that part of the world will present numerous business opportunities.

One post-MBA career path I am considering is international product and venture strategy in emerging markets. Success in this area requires entrepreneurial approaches to identify promising opportunities, sharp project management skills, cross-cultural team experience and an enterprise view of the business. An MBA will help build upon the skills acquired from my Datasage and Ford experiences and provide me with a framework for assessing business in an enterprise context. If I return to the auto industry, I will need to be able to determine whether or not the projected strength of the yen will make a Japanese supply base viable for a Malaysian assembly plant. Perhaps from an investment strategy standpoint, I must learn to prioritize investing my company's money to develop a unique product for India over continued development of profitable North American sport utility vehicles. In a five-year time frame, I will leverage my enterprise skills in the role of a program manager, leading a cross-cultural product development team that may conduct engineering work in North America or Europe with manufacturing and sales in East Asia.

Tying Two Missions Together

The mission statement of the Harvard Business School is: To educate leaders who make a difference in the world. Martin R. Curiel took this statement to heart, making connections between Harvard's mission statement and his own. This can be helpful for questions about what you can bring to a school.

When researching Harvard and writing his essays, Martin first looked at the school's mission statement and then broke it down into pieces. He asked himself how he was a leader and what he planned to do in the future to develop his leadership. He analyzed how he has made a difference. He also thought about his personal mission statement, which is to use his abilities and resources to benefit his community.

"You really want to look at that mission statement, understand what it says and try to project your experiences, motivations and desires to tie them to the mission statement," he says.

When writing his essays, Martin used Harvard's and his own mission statement to guide which experiences and strengths to highlight to the school. He believes it makes a difference to show how the two relate.

"Everyone's experiences are different, but if you can tie your experiences into what the school is trying to do, you'll increase your chances of getting in," he says. His strategy worked since he's now a student at Harvard Business School.

A Wharton MBA focused on multinational management along with an MA in International Studies from the Lauder Institute will serve as the ideal bridge connecting my technical automotive experience in product development to a career in international product and venture strategy. Wharton/Lauder's student population, diverse in both its ethnic make-up and business backgrounds, presents an attractive environment for me as I feel I have learned equally from peers as I have from my academic and professional experiences. Born in Buenos Aires, Argentina and raised in rural Canada and the metropolitan east coast of the United States, I feel that I can contribute to Wharton's Learning Team philosophy by sharing my cultural perspectives as well as my interests in business management.

I also look forward to building new relationships in Lauder's international community, just as I have maintained collegial relationships with my Horiba colleagues during annual Society of Automotive Engineer conventions over the past five years. Finally, the joint program curriculum, including opportunities abroad to build my language skills to a professionally capable level, offers me a chance to catalyze great ideas into high-growth, global ventures.

After graduation from the Lauder Institute, I will be armed with superior foreign language skills and greater cultural sensitivity. These aptitudes will enable me to lead cross-cultural teams in an increasingly interdependent global economy. Years from now, I hope to get off a plane after forging my first new venture partnership in the developing East Asian economy and reflect on all the learning and teamwork that went into filling in the second eye of my dharma idol.

Richard A. Delgado
Cox School of Business at Southern Methodist University

In a recent employee newsletter I wrote, "Change will be the only constant in the deregulated energy marketplace of the future. As natural gas and electric industries continue to converge into what will be the largest commodity-driven industry in the world, opportunities for success will abound with market victories going to those companies who are agile enough to adapt their corporate cultures." Of course, what I should have written is, "Changing a corporation's culture is much easier said than done, for there are no right or wrong answers . . .only right or wrong decisions."

As a member of a joint Columbia/NiSource merger integration team, I have learned the hard way that there is nothing soft about the process of cultural change. The business lessons an acquired company must endure can be just as hard as the marketplace itself. Yet, it is here, at the intersection of cultural change and business decision, that I believe my professional calling is rooted. Whether as a consultant re-engineering global processes or as an informed manager directing domestic operations, I know that managing organizational development is my ultimate career goal.

A career implementing organizational change is a direct reflection of my personal interest and the logical extension of my professional experience. Over three years ago, I came to Columbia as one of 16 analysts (undergraduates) and associates (MBAs) recruited to participate in rotational-based management development program know as STEP. It was the expressed mission of the STEP pool to bring new talent, fresh ideas and innovation to evolving and transforming a company emerging from bankruptcy. From communications to commercial services, I moved from rotation to rotation searching for stretch experiences that would enable me to apply my skills and focus my imagined career path. During each of these rotations, I enjoyed a broad range of functional responsibility, yet always knew that I was more interested in the subtext of our internal business practices—the subtleties of organizational development, interpersonal relationships and the belief systems which informed them.

As a STEP associate evaluating marketing synergies throughout the company, I was close enough to the fire to see how the cumulative effects of downsizing, the introduction of new management and the fear of the unknown devalued our cultural capital. Now, as a manager directing communications and overseeing the dissemination of information, I have the greater responsibility of actively defining our evolving culture. Although my managerial status affords me greater knowledge about organizational dilemmas, in this stage of my professional development I am unable to connect all the dots necessary to effect meaningful change. In the context of organizational learning, I have reached a natural fork in the road, and therefore need a professional training that will allow me to process my real world experiences and answer some of the questions I have already begun to ask.

Given my career interest in organizational development, I briefly entertained the idea of pursing an advanced degree in the discipline. After exploring various organizational development programs, I concluded that while a formal behavioral science education provided excellent insight into organizational management, it did not offer the core business skills required to effectively manage organizations. Consequently, my decision to pursue an MBA is driven not only by the professional applicability of the credential but by the degree's ability to unite personal interests with a broad professional focus that values and rewards my previous marketing and communications experience.

While many MBA programs will increase my functional competence and develop business specific aptitudes, I decided to apply to SMU because of the unique philosophy that is the Cox Advantage. Through research into the Cox School of Business and discussions with current students, I have become keenly aware of SMU's unwavering commitment to innovation, globalism, corporate interaction, class intimacy and hands-on learning to create a supportive learning environment that is unmatched in terms of student satisfaction and placement. It is obvious that the Cox School's commitment to students, faculty and the business community-at-large is the cornerstone of a truly unique and rewarding educational experience.

Ultimately, I am confident that my maturity of character, intellectual hunger and professional experience have prepared me for the discipline and sophistication a Cox MBA will merit. In what I know to be the next logical step in the refinement of my career direction, I am positive that receiving a strong grounding in the financial, strategic and operational systems which inform management theory and practice will make me a wiser manager today and a more effective change agent tomorrow.

Anonymous
Haas School of Business at the University of California at Berkeley

My professional goal is to attain a senior role in the real estate consulting industry within the next eight years. I feel that an MBA committed to real estate is critical to realizing this ambition. The ideal MBA would provide hands-on field experience through student-initiated projects, offer courses and development in a wide range of real estate topics and offer resources and facilities that show its commitment to staying on the cutting edge of the real estate industry. There is no doubt that I can find such an ideal MBA at Haas.

My background stems from accounting and finance. After I graduated from the NYU Stern Undergraduate School of Business, I joined Ernst & Young (E&Y) and specialized in the financial services industry. I enjoyed working in the finance industry because it was both analytical and fast-paced. After two years of auditing, I was invited to join Credit Suisse First Boston (CSFB) by a former supervisor who found me an excellent opportunity in the CSFB real estate product control group. I was attracted to the opportunity because I would learn about a new product, obtain exposure to a global business and report directly to a manager. I left E&Y ready to venture into the world of real estate.

Currently at CSFB, I have the exclusive responsibility of analyzing and monitoring multi-million dollar domestic and international real estate investment portfolios. I participate in weekly disposition meetings to discuss the status and exit strategies of distressed assets and then work closely with support groups such as risk and credit management, operations and financial control to ensure that the transactions are completed efficiently and accurately. Since these portfolios contain distressed assets that are no longer performing and recovery seems unlikely, they require daily analysis and monitoring. Upper management and regulatory agencies

How Recruiting Can Help You Pick the Right School

It was not enough for Allan Boomer to know that Merrill Lynch recruited at the University of Rochester. He also needed to know what kind of recruiting they did at the school. When he found out that they focused on operations and his field was finance, he knew that the school was not a good fit.

"Nine-tenths of the battle is being on a company's recruiting list," says Allan, now a student at NYU's Stern School of Business, adding, "But when I looked at the companies that recruited at the schools and peeled the onion just a little bit more, I saw a mismatch."

He recommends that you don't just look at the list of companies that recruit at a prospective business school but also at what they recruit for. This will help you find a better match.

are constantly questioning and reviewing the portfolio. The volatile market and recent world affairs have made it even more critical for me to be fully on-board with any events that may impact the portfolio. As a result, my role in the real estate product control group can be fairly demanding.

My involvement with the real estate portfolios and my interaction with various top managers in different real estate functions have shown me that there are many facets to the real estate business. The business involves analyzing risk and exposure, assessing legal and tax implications and evaluating the latest trends in the real estate industry. Real estate is not an industry that one can easily jump into and learn on the job. It is an industry best learned through a classroom setting that combines lectures and case studies with interactive projects led by professionals who can apply business strategies to real estate. In addition, while I feel that the opportunities I have been afforded at CSFB provide ample exposure to real estate asset investments, I have limited exposure to other aspects of the business such as real estate finance and securitizations, ecommerce and urban development. These are areas I would like to explore and make part of my MBA curriculum.

There is no question that the MBA Real Estate Program at the Haas School of Business is one of the nation's top programs and offers incomparable resources at the Fisher Center for Real Estate and Urban Economics. The annual Real Estate and Economics Symposium sponsored by the research center is further evidence of the Haas dedication and commitment to excellence in the real estate industry. I hope that Haas will help me lay the groundwork upon which I can build my career in real estate.

ESSAYS

Why Attend Our School?

IN MANY WAYS THE ADMISSION OFFICER IS A MATCHMAKER who is trying to find the right fit between applicant and school. Each school has a different ideology, approach to teaching, strengths in curriculum and social offerings. Because they are so different, business schools often ask what appeals to you about their school and how it fits your needs. Business schools want to be sure that you are not only adding value to their campuses but also that they can offer you the right education that will fulfill your goals.

To answer this type of question, you will first need to do some research on the schools. Read the schools' brochures, websites and catalogs. To get more information from students' perspectives, dig a little deeper by looking at the school's student-produced publications and students' personal websites.

One of the best ways to research business schools is to visit them. Take a tour of the campus, sit in on some classes and meet with professors. Also spend some time with current students, attend a social hour or club meeting and have lunch or coffee to discuss what it's like to be a student there.

As you write about why you'd like to attend a particular school, you can use your firsthand observations. This not only demonstrates that you understand how your background will match the school but is also evidence of your desire to attend it. Explain what you have learned from your research, what you would like to take away from specific professors' classes or research and how you see yourself fitting into the school.

Be sure to describe how your background matches what the school seeks and how your professional goals can be met by the school.

leadership?

anticipate
contributing to TUSM
community?

is there anything else we should
know about you?

Essays: Why Attend Our School?

Anonymous
Harvard Business School

In politics, science and business, the well-being of a society depends largely on the quality and effectiveness of its leaders. It is in the best interest of all to ensure that we develop and nurture the best people to take on the many leadership roles required in our society. My life dream, and the primary reason for my desire to attend Harvard Business School, is to lead an organization that will focus on seeking out and developing potential leaders.

In the midst of our inner-city neighborhoods, poor rural communities and migrant farm labor camps reside many talented young students. Yet due to many factors, many of these individuals perpetuate the cycle of poverty and low achievement. My mission in life is to help awaken the leadership potential within them, not only by inspiring them through my personal story, but also by helping them obtain the appropriate resources and develop the necessary skills that will allow them to make "quantum leaps."

Initiating a non-profit corporation has allowed me to create and test the business model I plan to use. My engineering career has helped me develop the technical and analytical skills key to managing a business. HBS will provide me with additional management tools, resources and, more importantly, leadership abilities to achieve my dream of developing thousands of future leaders nationwide.

Furthermore, I believe in the HBS teaching model whereby students teach each other through shared experiences and perspectives. I look forward to learning extensively from my classmates, listening to their philosophies of how we should deal with current and future challenges. Similarly, I hope to broaden the horizons of my cohorts through my life story. My career as an operations engineer, my work initiating a non-profit corporation and my life as a poor farmworker will add a unique perspective to their business school experience.

Jeff Marquez
Anderson School at UCLA

My long-term career goal is to be a Chief Strategy Officer for a multinational media company. To this end, my short-term objective is to join a strategic consulting firm, focusing on the entertainment and media arenas. Through practical exposure to a variety of media companies in strategic consulting, I will gain an understanding of the complexities involved in this sector. By attending the Anderson School, I believe I will sharpen my intellectual ability and further develop the strategic skills required to successfully fulfill my goals.

I believe my skills and interests are well suited for a strategic career within the media sector. I excel at determining long-term goals and adopting a course of action to carry out those goals. Furthermore, both as a participant and as a spectator, I have always found joy in the entertainment arena and have often used it as a creative outlet. The extremely competitive nature of this industry, combined with a continuous, yet unpredictable environment, further enhances my interest. In addition, the media's powerful reach has always intrigued me. As a CSO in this sector, I intend on using my skills, education and creative interests to explore new forums and distribution methods in an effort to extend good feelings to a larger number of people.

Although I have gained substantial experience as a consultant for the Information, Communication and Entertainment practice of PricewaterhouseCoopers, I recognize that my focus has revolved around information technology. My experience has not adequately prepared me for broader strategic issues. At Anderson, I intend to gain a more in-depth understanding of business disciplines and thus gain confidence in areas of business for which I have had limited exposure.

The superior curriculum offered at the Anderson School will provide a "real life" business-oriented education that will enhance my personal and professional growth. In addition to Anderson's core curriculum, entertainment electives such as "Strategic Management in the Entertainment Industry" and "Positioning in the Changing Entertainment Landscape" will give me the basic analytical and conceptual tools necessary to formulate business strategies in my future endeavors. During my recent visit to Professor William Cockrum's "Managing Finance and Financing the Emerging Enterprise" class, I was able to observe the energetic student-professor interaction and the unparalleled learning environment of the Anderson School. These factors coupled with the engaging conversations that I had with students and faculty fuel my enthusiasm to attend Anderson.

Lesser-Known Sources of Information about Business Schools

After you've read the brochures and web-sites, you might think you know everything you possibly can about your prospective business schools. But remember that most applicants read the same sources and have the same information. When it comes to the question of why you want to attend a specific school, it's crucial that you go beyond the usual sources.

"Often, this is a trick question to find out if you have done your homework," says Peter Gasca, a student and admission inter-viewer at Georgetown's McDonough School of Business. He says, "It is essential to know the school beyond what you find in the school brochure or on the school's website."

You can find out more about business schools by visiting them, meeting current students and professors, sitting in on classes and observing the atmosphere of the campus. If you can't visit, then you can attend information sessions that the business schools give. Most schools have information sessions in the major met-ropolitan areas across the country and internationally as well.

To get the real scoop, Allan Boomer, a student at NYU's Stern School, says to read the student publications. He says, "Most student newspapers are pretty unbiased because the audience is not prospective students but actual students. They're going to be objective."

I believe the knowledge that I will gain through interacting with highly motivated students and prominent faculty members will be as important in influencing my career development as anything that I will learn in the classroom. Participating in the Producer's Program of the School of Film & Television and joining the Entertainment Management Association will be a terrific introduction to fellow colleagues interested in the media sector. Furthermore, the international climate of the Anderson School will allow me to continue to learn in a multi-cultural environment and thus provide me with a broader perspective on business and life.

Changes in globalization and technology continue to challenge the strategic direction of the entertainment and media sectors. Managers are faced with the complexity of an industry with high levels of ambiguity. What affect will advances in technology have on a company's ability to distribute content efficiently and effectively to a broader audience? How will international markets influence change in an era of increased competition and convergence? In order to successfully maneuver an international media company in today's difficult environment, a leader needs to draw on his educational background and experience to answer these questions. My experience and comfort with these forces compounded by Anderson's global perspective will allow me to easily adapt and anticipate such radical changes to the industry.

The opportunities and benefits offered through the Anderson School are unique. With a diverse curriculum, a strong entertainment presence and a prominent faculty alumni base, the Anderson School program is exceptionally suited to my short-term and long-term career objectives. The combination of personal and professional development offered by the Anderson School at UCLA represents a platform that I can build upon for the rest of my life.

Student Aid: How Current B-School Students Can Help

You can get a lot of help from current business school students. Even one that you've just met, says Saul A. Lopez, a recent graduate of Wharton at the University of Pennsylvania.

On his way home from visiting Wharton during the prospective student day, he and another fellow applicant ran into a second year student. Even though they had never met, the student spent time speaking with them about the application process and volunteered to help read their essays. Saul thought it was a polite gesture, but he says, "I was pleasantly surprised when he kept his commitment to a complete stranger." He says that the helpfulness of this student was one of the reasons he decided to attend Wharton.

Gabriel Freund also received help from a current student. He says, "Thank God I had a great current MBA student who worked in the admission committee look at my essays and tell me to revise them and sell myself more." He said that before the help, his essays rambled. It helped as he's now a student at the University of Michigan Business School.

Ruben Sigala
Harvard Business School

As a senior consultant in the financial services industry, I have participated in the management of client engagements and in executive discussions regarding the general business objectives of the organization. These experiences have contributed greatly in determining my professional goals. My ultimate career objective is to obtain an executive consulting position that would initially focus on managing individual client relations with an eventual focus on directing overall market strategy. Although I am currently working in my desired field, supplementing my professional experience with an MBA from Harvard would provide unparalleled training for the daily challenges I would encounter in this role.

Harvard's case method of instruction is analogous to many of the circumstances inherent in any consulting project. Often, the challenge of the consultant is to develop cogent solutions to complex issues in which information is limited and incomplete. Harvard's case studies focus directly on these scenarios and would serve to develop a refined expertise in methodologies required to efficiently and appropriately service consulting clients.

Further, Harvard's section based structure would serve to enhance my ability to interact and function within an environment of diverse influences and operational methods. The ability to efficiently integrate within unfamiliar corporate cultures is fundamental to the value a consultant brings to the client. Cultivating my ability within Harvard's challenging environment will greatly expand the breadth of client relationships I could manage.

Finally, Harvard's general management focus will provide the perfect forum to supplement quantitative coursework with strategic and managerial studies. This will provide practical preparation for evaluating critical factors necessary to advance an organization's position within a dynamic market.

These attributes, taken in conjunction with many other incomparable benefits, such as access to the Harvard networking community and the credential associated with a Harvard degree, would provide the perfect springboard to meet my professional goals.

Dan Gertsacov
Harvard Business School

My experiences over the past five years promoting corporate social responsibility in Latin America have proven to me that we are evolving towards becoming a global society that will judge a company not only based on its financial returns, but also on its social and environmental impacts. I am focused now and through to the future on preparing companies and enterprises to reap the benefits of these larger societal trends.

My career goals are to act as a social entrepreneur, using market mechanisms to make the world a better place. I intend to launch and manage for-profit enterprises that simultaneously serve the needs of markets and society, developing products that go beyond just satisfying the demands of the consumer, but go a step further and attempt to help heal the planet and mend our society.

During a recent visit to Boston, I had the pleasure of meeting a number of students, as well as leading Harvard Business School professors in my field of interest, including Dr. James Austin and Dr. Allen Grossman, specialists in social enterprise. They helped me realize that Harvard Business School would be the best learning environment for me to advance in my career goals, with the school providing a strong academic foundation in management, combined with inspiration and challenges from accomplished peers and faculty members.

I have a clear vision of the world that I see as possible—a world that I intend to be a leader in creating, through business and social enterprise. From top-level management training to the interactions and innovative synergies achieved between peers, I strongly believe that Harvard Business School can provide me with an opportunity that would prove vital in my quest to move the business world, and our world in general, in a very positive direction.

Anthony M. Fernandez
Harvard Business School

Each of my professional experiences to date has driven a part of my current career aspirations. My engineering internships revealed my interest in manufacturing and technology-based industries, while my consulting experience has uncovered a strong interest in the managerial and strategic aspects of business. In the near future, I hope to combine these interests through a managerial position within a manufacturing or technology-based company. My long-term goals are focused on taking my managerial position to the executive and entrepreneurial levels.

These are two major gaps I need to fill in order to truly excel in my desired future professional roles. First and foremost, I need to establish a new way of thinking. Too often I apply an engineering mindset to business problems. I must complement my current mentality with a way of thinking that includes a better understanding of the big picture. Ultimately, this will allow me to more effectively recognize, develop and take advantage of business opportunities. Second, I need to become more well rounded in my business knowledge. Increased exposure in the areas of marketing, finance and international business is critical to the leadership positions I hope to obtain in the future.

The MBA experience is undoubtedly the most effective way to address these career needs, and I view Harvard as the ideal place to obtain this experience. The quality of the HBS students is what appeals to me most. Interacting with such a talented, diverse and experienced group of professionals will foster unparalleled career and personal growth. Furthermore, the case method draws me to Harvard. To me, the case method provides the most effective way to obtain a business education. Last and certainly not least, I value Harvard's focus on leadership. My professional experience has taught me that the most successful people in the business world are those who can effectively lead others. Attending HBS will enable me to build upon the leadership skills that will be crucial throughout my future career.

Valerie R. Ramirez
Wharton School at the University of Pennsylvania

An important tool for public sector leaders in the future will surely be the utilization of information technology. The speed and scope of change in technology have created special challenges as well as opportunities for public leaders committed to excelling in a new era of management—the information age. Specifically, I believe that governments can benefit from working closely with private industry to learn new ways to deliver public services. This translates into a tremendous opportunity for those individuals who help convert the public sector from a largely inefficient industry to a more customer-oriented, information-driven industry. I want not only to focus and participate in this future but also to actively shape its course by applying private sector-based solutions to the problems confronted by the public sector. I hope to shape this exciting future by first working as a strategy consultant and then, eventually, moving into a senior management position within the public sector.

I first became interested in the public sector while I was an undergraduate at UC Berkeley. In addition to my public policy studies, I worked as an intern with my U.S. congressman, William Baker. After gaining the trust of Congressman Baker in my two years as a volunteer, I was promoted to lead campaign manager. In the capacity as one of the only paid workers on the campaign, I was responsible for initiatives that resulted in a powerful grassroots organization with over 5,000 volunteers. In addition to my campaign activities, I also helped draft legislation ranging from privatizing the Department of Education to reducing the capital gains tax. This work had a profound impact on my view that public agencies could benefit greatly from incorporating private sector strategies into the operations of the public sector. After our campaign was narrowly defeated, I decided to pursue an opportunity with the corporate communications/government relations group of a large oil and gas company, Tosco Refining Company. While satisfying my interest to work with government agencies, I was also attracted by the opportunity to initiate an internal intranet system that would disseminate company wide news across a network. Through my efforts, this intranet system eventually allowed managers across the country to access a single database and create solutions to news impacting the company.

After gaining several years of public-private sector experience, I decided to pursue a Master's in public policy and administration from the School of International and Public Affairs at Columbia University. While at Columbia, I conducted research with two leading professors considering methods to integrate e-commerce (e-government) technology at the national level. After completing this research project, I continued to focus on the public sector and information technology by accepting an internship with the New York City Department of Finance. In my capacity as intern, I worked closely with IBM senior consultants to propose innovative methods to access a wide range of municipal services and information through the Internet. Based on my performance with the IBM team, I was offered a position with IBM Global Consulting Services to return to the New York City client site as the lead government consultant.

Today, I am leading a team of business analysts and technical consultants to design an information system that will allow administrative law judges to conduct hearings online. During this lengthy engagement, I have had the opportunity to gain firsthand insights from New York City public leaders about the future demand for e-government services. I have learned that before many public agencies can incorporate a truly e-government environment, they will require a complete reconfiguration of the equipment and systems that are used to conduct business. Increasingly, this enormous investment will require that public leaders establish not only a short-term goal for transforming to an e-government environment but also a long-term plan for adapting to the future challenges that the information age is sure to bring. While my training at IBM Global Consulting Services has provided me with implementation experience in this emerging e-government market, I have not been exposed to broader strategy projects that examine the overall business environment. These skills will be important in helping me pursue my next career objective—working at a strategy consulting firm on e-government related issues.

I am particularly excited about these career opportunities because in the next few years public leaders will increasingly rely on non-traditional sources for advice and services to deliver e-government solutions to their constituents. I eagerly seek to be a part of this emerging market by serving as a strategy consultant providing specialized strategic consulting services to local, state, national, and international governments. With less than 1 percent of governments currently offering e-government capabilities, the next 10 years will present enormous opportunities to advise public agencies to adapt such strategies. Both my academic exposure and my job experiences have provided me with an excellent foundation in which to be a future leader in this emerging market. However, in order to truly implement the private sector reforms that are needed in the public sector, I will need to augment my public sector skills with a broad business education that emphasizes private sector solutions. Although I am excited about the opportunity to be a strategy consultant, I hope to eventually return to the public sector in a leadership position. In this role, I hope to use my strategic consulting experience and Wharton MBA to initiate meaningful and lasting change to the operation and e-government strategies within the public sector.

To move forward with my career plan, I now need to develop the strategic management skills that a rigorous Wharton business education can provide. With its strengths in strategic management and the newly developed e-commerce major, Wharton offers an ideal opportunity in which to build my knowledge base in strategic management and information technology. I believe, however, a complete business school education must go beyond coursework and include interaction with faculty, business leaders and other students. More than any other business school, Wharton has the resources to offer this complete business school education. The recently developed West Trek will offer me the opportunity to interact with Internet and other technology business leaders. In addition, the Zweig lecture series offers students the opportunity to attend a lecture and meet successful business leaders. After hearing about visits from Jack Welch and Warren Buffett, I am eager to participate in a program that will continue to attract influential business leaders to campus.

Beyond the academic resources available at Wharton, I've also grown to appreciate the other factors that make Wharton one of the best business schools in the country. Because my older brother has been at Wharton for the past two years, I have had the opportunity to gain a unique insight into the students and administration at the school. After visiting my brother on numerous occasions, I have come to appreciate Wharton's team-based culture that encourages learning in a more relaxed setting and creates a very collegial social environment. The learning team program, the FAP course and the numerous social events serve as testament to the team-based environment at Wharton. I also appreciate the entrepreneurial environment that appears everywhere at the school. I am amazed at the level of participation in the E-Club and the other clubs that promote entrepreneurial activity on campus.

As I prepare for business school, I hope to bring my passion, knowledge and in-depth vision of the technological evolution occurring in the public sector to the students at the Wharton School. I wish to share my views that public agencies, whether they be domestic or international, have the potential to radically alter the way they deliver services. I believe the Wharton School is the ideal setting in which to work with others from a variety of different backgrounds to help resolve the financial, technological and global challenges of the public agencies of tomorrow. This can begin by attending the Wharton School, where I can enrich the educational and social environment and simultaneously continue on my path of becoming a leader in the public sector.

Allan Boomer
New York University Stern School of Business

After years of preparation and months of scrutinizing MBA programs throughout the world, my journey to success has brought me to New York University. Initially, it was Stern's academic reputation, strong entrepreneurial curriculum and geographic proximity to the major financial markets that attracted me. In the end, it was Opportunity that confirmed my decision.

I desire an MBA experience that will be the most memorable and worthwhile venture of my life. The degree itself will provide the education necessary to leverage my professional experience and expedite the achievement of my life's goal of being an entrepreneur. Realizing the gravity associated with choosing a school that would be well aligned with my goals, I spent a substantial amount of time evaluating business schools around the world. In October, I experienced Stern firsthand. During the AHBBS Career Fair, I conversed with Stern graduates, current students, a corporate CEO and a number of high-ranking executives. The conference bolstered Stern's high standing by poignantly addressing the subject of "Leading Through Change" and exposing me to minority students poised to lead major corporations, as well as successful business magnates who attribute their success to Stern.

Surprisingly, the most revealing part of my Stern experience was actually my train-ride home. I passed the time perusing the aptly named student newspaper, Opportunity. I always make it a point to read student newspapers because they offer a raw, unbiased university perspective, unlike the sparkling, politically-correct marketing brochures produced by admissions offices. I found Opportunity to be no ordinary periodical of the student body, thus an even more lucid confirmation that Stern is no ordinary business school.

My research of business school newspapers has led me to believe many are regurgitated collections of boring, poorly-written articles about trite topics like "Business School Is So Tough, Yet Rewarding," student / faculty profiles, club activities and career fairs. Opportunity, however, contains well-written articles that tackle a wide breadth of student-centered issues, like competing in a tough job market, U.S. foreign wartime policy, and ethics in management coupled with light-hearted humor in pieces about the New York supermarket experience and "businesspeak," the vague and optimistic vernacular of corporate executives. I was also pleasantly surprised to find several community-related articles that explore the vast offerings of the Big Apple and detail volunteer opportunities.

Why Allan Boomer?

Opportunity introduced me to two organizations that I would both give to and gain from—the Urban Business Assistance Corporation (UBAC) and the Entrepreneurs Exchange. My experience in marketing, operations and finance would enable me to add value to these organizations, while my need to grow and practice in the ways of entrepreneurship will be served simultaneously. I am especially excited about UBAC because its mission of helping minority businesses is perfectly aligned with my dream of running a venture capital / consulting firm that focuses on minority business interests. The fact that the UBAC has been around for more than 30 years indicates Stern's long-term commitment to the diversity of its business community. In addition to these two groups, I intend to place my byline on many articles within Opportunity. While in college, I was the sports editor of the student newspaper and my love for writing has never ceased.

It is evident from my visits and interactions with students and alumni at the NYU campus that Stern is a place where the world is an integral part of the classroom. Advantageously, my experience at Merrill Lynch would position me as an asset to classroom discussions, as I have held various leadership positions at this multi-trillion dollar brokerage firm, all the while absorbing its strategic vision. My propensity for guiding and aiding others will place me in many situations that will improve the quality of life at Stern, which stems from my dedication to working in the community and assuming leadership roles. I have piloted several collegiate volunteer initiatives, mentored children, taught workshops and represented my university as its Official Student Ambassador. My desire is to have an even greater upshot at Stern.

My life's goal is to help others while creating wealth through an entrepreneurial venture in the financial services industry. In college, I learned how to market my business. At Merrill Lynch, I learned how to manage the day-to-day operations of my business. At NYU, I expect the lessons to come full-circle as my acumen grows more keen. Stern is the right school, and New York is the right place. I'm ready. All I need now is the right opportunity.

ESSAYS

What Do You Offer?

IN BUSINESS SCHOOL YOU WILL LEARN AS MUCH from the students sitting to your right and left as you will from your professors' lectures. A large part of your education will come from your fellow students.

Business school admission officers know this and thus want to create a class of students who have diverse backgrounds and who can contribute to their own education. This is why they ask for you to describe in your own words what you bring to the school.

This question requires some introspection, some thoughts about what makes you, well, you. If you don't describe your business experience in the other essays that you are writing, you will probably want to describe it here. Your work experience and what you have gained from it is one of the most important factors in business school admission. But if you have described your work experience elsewhere, you can look at other aspects of what you have to share.

Think about activities that you have been involved in, experiences that you have had or some of your accomplishments. These can all give the business schools a more well-rounded picture of what you will bring.

Again, focus on those qualities that are unique to you so that you can distinguish yourself from other students.

Essays: What Do You Offer?

Armando De Casas
USC Marshall School

It was 8 a.m. on Monday and my mind was full of a million questions. How would understanding a master production schedule impact my life today? Would knowing how to calculate economic order quantities come in handy? Am I going to be okay? I remember feeling sure of my proficiency in quantitative methods used to evaluate the soundness of manufacturing processes. Surely, I thought, these skills would be the foundation of my success in the manufacturing industry. The reader of this narrative might misconstrue my uncertainty and believe that I was facing a college senior's greatest fear, not having a job lined up after graduation. But the reality of the situation was much worse. The day that I am recounting is my first day at work, my first job as a college graduate.

I pulled into the LG Inc. parking lot at 7:45 a.m. and sat in my own private office—complete with all of the perks that accompany such a luxury. I was fresh out of college. Why the panic? I was a production supervisor. This meant that I wouldn't be able to rely on a keyboard or fancy software to get things accomplished. To the 35 individuals outside my factory office, technology was irrelevant.

Just 15 minutes into my employment at LG, I was astounded by one of my employees. "Buenos dias, Don Armando, bienvenido," Victoria uttered. The use of the Spanish word "Don" is a more formal version of the title mister. Up until that moment, the use of this term had always been reserved for people like my father and other men who personified experience and wisdom. I realized that Olivia and Esperanza, my group leaders, had 45 years of experience between them. Surely they awaited my revolutionary management techniques. I also noticed that 34 of the 35 employees in the department were women. Of these women, 90 percent of them were old enough to have been my mother. There I stood, faced with a challenge that had never been addressed with any depth in any of my business classes. How was I going to lead this group of individuals and achieve the desired results? Thumbing through the pages of a Frederick Taylor management book would be futile. During the last school quarter, one month earlier, I had been a successful softball manager. But I knew that telling my employees to hustle down the first base line would not be effective. Besides, LG's employee manual prohibited the use of baseball cleats on the factory floor.

I walked out to the factory floor with a notepad in hand and wondered what awaited me. I met with Olivia. I introduced myself and proceeded to ask questions for the next two hours, specifically, about processes such as what raw materials we used and how we loaded them into our machines. I had hoped to accomplish two things during those two hours: to learn the department and, more importantly, to convey that the success of the department would depend on the strength of our relationships.

Throughout my employment at LG, I learned many valuable lessons from this dynamic group of women. They taught me a great deal about work ethic, demonstrated by their dedication to the 6 a.m. morning shift and working overtime with short notice. Feedback was important because it demonstrated my interest in them by valuing the contributions each of them made to the department. This helped me gain their respect and allowed me to flourish as their leader. Though their pay was modest, their effort was anything but modest. I sought to be responsive with my employees as I would with any member of my family. I understood their concerns. Many of the issues affecting them existed in my own family. I derived great satisfaction from the team-based decision-making process. Ultimately, I made the final decision, but it came after careful consideration of more than one perspective. My investment in creating an environment that encouraged communication and an exchange of ideas was a determining factor in my success as a leader.

Eventually, I was able to incorporate my educational background into the department. Many of the production principles had been applicable since day one, but first I needed the employees to embrace my vision. I gained great satisfaction from instituting new processes. I made sure everyone understood why something needed to be changed or how a new process would improve our operations. For those who exhibited a desire for additional responsibility, the implementation of new processes was a welcomed sight. A firm believer in developing my employees, I would assign different tasks to overachieving employees and expose them to other aspects of the department. Employees who had been performing the same duties for 20 years were now able to learn the process of cycle counting and scrap reporting. I created new positions with different pay scales to give my employees a sense of opportunity. Many took advantage of such positions and were able to increase their incomes in the process. In the end, each of us understood our roles and the strength of our department illustrated how success depended on the collaborative effort of each individual. This crucial awareness was the first and most important lesson of my business career to date, for every element of the business cycle hinges on the presence of interpersonal relationships. I would not have been able to manage 68 employees had I not come to this realization.

Perhaps the single life experience that has impacted both my personal and professional careers is the uniqueness of my position in my social environment. The position of which I speak is the series of "firsts" that I have fulfilled: the first member of my extended family to have received a college education, the first born child in my immediate family and being a first generation Mexican-American. Growing up in the city of Pomona, California, the environment in which I was raised is one encumbered with the realities of immigrant life: modest incomes, language barriers and constant struggle. And it is this struggle that has provided me with the work ethic and motivation to succeed. I have always been a mediator in my world, a mediator of languages, cultures and, most importantly, of education. I have been an invaluable resource to my family, friends and co-workers because of all three factors. I always knew that an education was a source of social and economic empowerment, and because of that awareness, I made sure that I remained focused on studying. Had I not valued knowledge the way I do, I would not have been able to be as effective a translator for my parents, who do not speak English; I would not have been able to inspire my younger siblings to go to college; I would not have been able to understand the needs of my Hispanic co-workers and made them the productive employees that our employer demanded and I could not have been able to expose any of them to the information and opportunities that would ensure better lives for them all. Indeed, my versatile role as an educated Hispanic has made me a valuable leader to many, and had it not been for my social environment, perhaps those leadership skills would never have developed. I will bring this human approach to my MBA program and apply these principles whenever possible. I will make sure that my classmates look beyond quantitative factors when evaluating the condition of an organization. I hope that my classmates will benefit from my experience and be able to incorporate this perspective in their lives, both personally and professionally.

Linsey L. Herman
Kellogg School of Management at Northwestern

Until I went to culinary school, it was inconceivable to me that I had an elitist bone in my body. In high school and at Harvard, I prided myself on being an outsider and a rebel. During my college years, I immersed myself in art, volunteered at quirky cultural organizations, worked part-time jobs in interesting places and had intelligent friends who were just like me. I made movies and videos and contributed artwork to local comic books.

Showing How Nontraditional Backgrounds Fit with Business School

You may not see the immediate connection between a professional chef and business school, but Linsey Herman made sure that the schools that she applied to did. After graduating from Harvard College, she attended a culinary institute and became a professional chef in Boston.

She admits, "Business school was not an obviously logical step." But she made it one by describing her goals for what she would do after business school. She planned to use her education to learn how to start and operate a Parisian-style marketplace, a way to tie in retail business with her love of cooking. The business schools apparently understood the connection and Linsey was accepted by Northwestern's Kellogg School of Management.

While there are a lot of consultants and investment bankers in business schools, these are not the only professions that the schools seek. In fact, admission officers actively seek to build a class of students from different backgrounds because they know that a roomful of consultants will not learn as much from each other as a roomful of students from different industries.

"The classroom thrives on the fact that you may be sitting next to a guy who studied economics, a woman who studied English literature and a past Peace Corps member. It all adds to the flavor in the classroom," says Kristina L. Nebel, director of admissions and financial aid at the University of Michigan Business School.

Wenny Tung believed that she could use her nontraditional background to her advantage. She says, "I could bring something to the table that no one else could. I had a job that no one else had," she says.

Surely there were other applicants who had worked in similar fields as Wenny, which were operations and sales, but she also had a unique employer, Walt Disney World. She used her background to describe why she wanted to go to business school. While at Walt Disney World, she learned a lot about budgeting, but she wanted to enhance her experience in business school to work in marketing in the entertainment industry.

"I had to look at my strengths and weaknesses and learn how to sell myself to them. I was able to weave a story about why I was coming to business school," says Wenny, a recent graduate of Duke's Fuqua School of Business.

Just because you are not a management consultant or an investment banker does not mean that you have a lower chance of getting into business school. In fact, schools love students from diverse business backgrounds. The key is to make it crystal clear to the school how an MBA fits into your overall career goals and how your past experience is an asset to helping you achieve those goals.

I was different from my peers, I thought. I was of the people. I was more real than my classmates, the ones who aspired to control the economies of their various homelands and influence and shape the cultural landscape. I was special. And then I went to culinary school.

I can't imagine an experience as jarring to my self-perception than that of my first year in culinary school. My values were turned upside-down. It was neither non-conformity nor intelligence that succeeded in the kitchen; it was youth, it was talent, it was strength, it was stamina, speed and coordination. It had nothing to do with education, intelligence, money, background or life experience. My background was of little help to me here. Success required an entirely new skill set, a different sort of intelligence, a competitive drive that I did not know if I possessed and an openness to other people who in a past life I would have avoided. To learn how to survive in this environment, I befriended the 17-year-old vocational school graduates who comprised 20 percent of my class, the 23-year-old cooks who had been in the kitchen since high school and some of the older career-changers who were formerly police officers or nurses or house painters. No longer was a similar background, academic achievement, documented intelligence or the use of proper grammar in daily speech determining whom I would choose as friends. My new criteria were simple: I sought out kind, respectful and thoughtful people who were unselfish and possessed a work ethic equal to my own. Intelligence, I realized, had many forms, and for too many years my blindness to this fact had limited my experience and my friendships.

I spent the years following culinary school extracting myself from my personal history. I worked twice as hard as anyone else in the kitchen to avoid having Harvard barbs thrown my way. If I did anything haphazardly or slowly, my pampered Harvard background was probably to blame. If I said anything that seemed strange or overly educated to my kitchen colleagues, it was because I was that show-off from Harvard. At some work-places I didn't even mention that I had a college degree. It didn't always seem appropriate and often that knowledge brought out the worst in my co-workers. I wanted to be seen for who I was, for what I was capable of, for my creativity and skill in the kitchen, not for my education or my background. And over time I succeeded.

As a professional cook, I learned that status came from the professional resume and from the singular pursuit of the "foodie" lifestyle. A stint at Trotter's, an internship at the French Laundry or a stage in France added considerable credibility and respect. Diverse experiences were encouraged, and frequent job changes were expected in the industry. Vacations and free evenings spent in pursuit of the perfect meal or dining in legendary restaurants also lent a certain mystique to a cook. I embraced the lifestyle, growing my own organic vegetables during the summer, planning my vacations around great restaurants, joining and participating in every food-related group I could find and saving my salary for frequent fine dining experiences, where I always found inspiration. I spent nearly six years completely absorbed in the food world. I even dreamed about it. For the dedicated cook, work was a 24-hour job. It was the only way to attain culinary perfection.

I found, however, that I needed to extend my experience beyond the kitchen. I needed balance; I needed time for my new martial arts training, which was scheduled during evening hours when I was usually at work in the kitchen, and I needed to learn more about the business of food. I became a cheesemonger, a seller of cheese, in a brand-new retail market in a college neighborhood. My new job freed up my evenings and gave me invaluable business experience. It also made good use of my culinary background. I studied cheese, the latest trend in the culinary world, as if it were an academic subject; within a month I knew everything about the 350 cheeses in my shop. I used my food background to explain flavor and food matching to my customers and to help them plan their meals. I enjoyed educating my customers and my co-workers and even received a little publicity in the Atlanta Journal-Constitution and on a Food Network TV show. I was asked to teach cheese classes. When I went out to eat, I was frequently greeted by, "Hello, cheese lady!" I became friends with the local dining critics, an assortment of chefs and other food notables. Within six months I was the city's foremost authority on cheese. Because of my unusual specialization and my lucky timing, I had quickly attained a position in the local food scene that I could never have achieved in the kitchen in the same amount of time. My minor celebrity, however, wasn't as important to me as watching my customers, colleagues and friends catch my contagious enthusiasm for the unusual food products to which I introduced them.

Doing professionally what most people think of as only a hobby has made me more open, receptive and willing to look beyond the surface to see the best in others. In the process, I have become less judgmental and more aware that difference is something to seek out, not avoid, in others. I have re-examined my values and the resulting changes have significantly broadened my experiences and friendships and have permitted me greater professional and personal opportunity.

Richard A. Delgado
Southern Methodist University Cox School of Business

This question asked students to imagine that it is 10 years after they graduate from business school and to write an article about themselves that would appear in a major international publication.

Excerpt from The Wall Street Journal

ABC Energy International Appoints Delgado as Executive VP of International Marketing Operations

Houston, February 7, 2013 – ABC Energy International (NYSE:ABC) announced today that Richard Anthony Delgado, III has been appointed executive vice president of global energy marketing operations, effective February 1, 2013.

Delgado most recently served as vice president of ABC-Mexico, an ABC subsidiary engaging in a highly publicized joint venture with the recently privatized PEMEX. Delgado joined ABC in January 2008 and has been instrumental in ABC International's strategic growth and earnings recovery. Most notably, he has brokered several recent Latin American acquisitions that have solidified the company's power generation portfolio.

"Richard is a proven leader who brings ABC Energy a wealth of merger management and acquisition expertise as well as significant energy marketing experience in the global arena," said John Doe, chairman, president and chief executive officer. "As we continue to implement our growth strategies, he will be a major player driving the marketing strategy that will underlie our success."

Before joining ABC Energy, Delgado was a principal with Acme Consulting, Inc., which provided organizational development consulting services to international natural gas, electric and other energy firms. Over half of his 14-year career has been devoted to developing M&A change management strategies, international gas marketing capabilities and power brokering techniques.

Delgado began his business career with the Columbia Energy Group where he served in various wholesale and retail marketing positions for Columbia Gas Transmission Corporation and Columbia Gas of Virginia. Delgado also served as assistant deputy for policy analysis at the American Gas Association, making policy recommendations on deregulation of natural gas and electricity. He also served as a consultant for the Department of Energy and as an international policy fellow with the Environmental Protection Agency.

He received his bachelor's degree from Swarthmore College and an MBA from Southern Methodist University's Cox School of Business. Delgado also serves on the boards of several prominent civic and charitable organizations including Habitat for Humanity International and the Nature Conservancy.

Anthony M. Fernandez
Kellogg School at Northwestern University

A student at the Harvard Business School, Anthony wrote this essay for the Kellogg School, where he was also accepted.

Almost every aspect of my upbringing relates back to experiences with my father. My father left Colombia to come to the U.S. when has was 20 years old. Like most immigrants, he was forced to quickly learn how to make a living in a very unfamiliar environment. This challenge would not be his toughest, however; he was later forced to raise a 10-year-old son on his own. Following my parents' divorce, my father obtained full custody of me. Since that day, he has been the single most influential person in my life.

To my father's credit, I have learned to live by the values and customs of both American and Colombian culture. This bi-cultural background has been established through balancing my exposure to American culture in school with interactions among members of the Colombian side of my family, who later came to America to pursue the same opportunity my father had already seized. A culturally diverse student body is one of Kellogg's most notable strengths; I can build upon this strength through a bi-cultural background that I am very proud of and extremely eager to share with others. I look forward to providing knowledge and awareness of the Colombian culture and bringing an international perspective to class discussions and social interactions with fellow classmates. Additionally,

I plan to contribute to Kellogg's international community by becoming involved in the Latin American Business Association and by participating in a South American GIM trip.

My father's career as a sheet metal mechanic and carpenter was also a big influence in my upbringing. Whether it was helping him build a staircase, fix a car or put siding on a house, I was always intimately involved with his "hands-on" way of life. My experience with this way of life has allowed me to understand and relate to the "blue-collar" side of business throughout my early career, therefore forming a perspective that is often times underrepresented in professional settings. By bringing this perspective and associated experiences to Kellogg, I can provide fellow MMM classmates with knowledge they will find valuable towards becoming effective organizational leaders in a manufacturing environment. Through team projects, for instance, I can help fellow students understand how "getting out and circulating among the troops" is critical in order to gain credibility and, ultimately, buy-in for managerial decisions.

Through a unique combination of breadth and depth, my professional experience also allows me to make a significant contribution to the learning experience of others at Kellogg. My experience in consulting has allowed me to develop breadth of business knowledge through diverse professional roles across several major industries. During team projects, I would be able to offer valuable information not only on different information system technologies but also on the implementation of these technologies in several major industries. For example, I can share with fellow classmates the knowledge of how electronic commerce can be used to increase revenue and reduce costs in the food and beverage, telecommunications and entertainment industries. Management consulting has also enabled me to work hand-in-hand with major corporations to embrace and implement organizational changes. This experience allows me to provide knowledge that is helpful to students who will be making leadership decisions that require changes to their organization. During class discussions, for example, I can provide insight into how major corporations have successfully, and sometimes unsuccessfully, dealt with the internal implications of major business decisions such as system implementations, reorganizations, layoffs and mergers.

My prior professional experiences with Ford Motor Company and Barré Company, Inc. have given me in-depth knowledge in the area of high-volume manufacturing. This knowledge is particularly valuable to the MMM program, where students can directly leverage an understanding of the operational aspects of manufacturing to be more effective in managerial roles. Through group projects and class interactions, I can help others understand the processes and technology behind taking an idea from raw materials to a finished product.

I have always made it a priority to supplement my professional and academic experiences with extracurricular involvement. For example, I currently hold leadership roles on the philanthropic and social committees of IMPACT-Atlanta, the local branch of my company's nationwide culture organization. My responsibilities with IMPACT-Atlanta include managing the fall coed softball team, coordinating community service events and organizing corporate outings at local establishments. My participation and leadership in extracurricular activities will undoubtedly continue upon entering business school. By becoming involved with some of Kellogg's special interest clubs, such as Business with a Heart and the Golf Club, I will make a significant contribution to Kellogg's dynamic student community. Moreover, I look forward to evaluating and taking opportunities to start new special interest clubs that can add to the already impressive variety of student organizations at Northwestern.

I will combine the abovementioned professional and life experiences with a strong work ethic and good sense of humor to make a very positive overall impact on Kellogg's MMM program. I look forward to contributing to the very thing that makes the Kellogg environment so special—the learning that takes place from the diverse personal qualities and life experiences of others.

ESSAYS

Leadership

WHEN YOU LOOK AT THE HIGH-PROFILE GRADUATES of business schools, you realize that they really are training the country's future business leaders. This is why business schools ask about your leadership experience. They want students who are going to make an impact in the business world.

Before you start answering the leadership question, consider what you want to convey about your philosophy of leadership and your leadership style. Your personal approach should come across through your answer.

Try to include an example from work if possible. This will show how you manage goals and people in a work environment. You can describe how you've been a leader even if you weren't officially managing employees. Perhaps you led a cross-departmental task force or you headed up a special project at work. Even though you didn't have official direct reports, you did work as a leader in these situations.

As you are describing your leadership experience, try to be as specific as possible. Explain why you made the decisions that you did, especially if they were difficult decisions. Outline your approach to leadership and what skills you try to exhibit when you are a leader. It is important to not just say that you are a leader but to show how you've actually led.

It is also important that you describe the results of your leadership. What were your successes? Did your group complete its project, did you make improvements for the company or did your team work well together? Provide tangible outcomes from your work.

One thing to keep in mind as you are writing an essay on leadership is that you should be careful not to take all of the credit or overinflate your accomplishments.

Essays: Leadership

Lyle B. Fogarty
University of North Carolina Kenan-Flagler Business School

Lyle wrote this essay role playing as the CEO of a local electronics store. It is a memo to his employees letting them know his strategy for competing against a national chain that is entering the market. A recent graduate of Emory University's Goizueta Business School, he wrote this essay for the Kenan-Flagler Business School, where he was also accepted.

To: All Employees

From: Lyle Fogarty, CEO

Subject: Adapting to a new environment

It is always my pleasure to look around and see what a great enterprise this team has built over the last two decades. In this competitive retail industry we have managed to excel continuously despite being one of the smaller players in the market. We have done so by repeatedly proving to our customers that they can depend on us for their home appliance and electronics needs. It has been our driving focus to exceed our customer expectations, and we have done so by being the most responsive to customer demands and offering exceptional value on our products. However, kudos for prior success can only propel us so far.

The surge of the Internet in the business and consumer marketplace could put us into a weakened market position if we do not formulate a quality electronic commerce plan and execute it rapidly. Our management team has been in place for several years, and we believe that this team has the ability to formulate a stellar plan that will lead us in the future. To complement the team's skills, we have added to the management team an e-commerce expert. With the hiring of William Beckles, we now have the necessary expertise and vision to lead our new e-commerce initiatives. A former executive at E-Toys, William brings a unique perspective since he has experience in a solely electronic commerce environment. His experience on best practices in this area will be of immense value to us as we integrate some of those practices into our retail outlets. Unlike E-Toys, we are, and anticipate always being, a retail business with retail outlets using technological advances to enhance our market position. While most of our similar sized competitors have not been able to keep pace with the market power of Circuit City and Best Buy, our strategy of controlled growth has kept us competitive. Many of you have met William during our strategy building sessions and he has indicated that our team has some excellent suggestions on how to integrate electronic solutions into our everyday business. It has been from the following vantage point that we have developed the bulk of our strategy—what e-commerce solutions will benefit our existing business relationships with customers and suppliers. The following synopsis of the plan was compiled by William and the E-commerce Solutions team.

We plan to begin implementation of each of the following initiatives within the next 90 days. During that time you may be asked to participate in beta tests, and we encourage you to accept and give critical feedback. As the strategy implementation progresses, all employees will attend a weeklong training session on the new tools available and how they will enhance our business. As always, we encourage any additional input you have. Like technology, our strategy is constantly evolving with the changing demands of our customers and market.

Tools Aimed at Improving Customer Service

The following tools are being developed as a means of accomplishing two of our primary objectives. First, these tools will help solidify our market position as the top provider of appliances and home electronics with regards to service and value. And second, buying from us is easy and fast.

Web Development - We have partnered with a web development and hosting service that is creating Fogartyelectronics.com. The web page has security features embedded in it, which protect our customers and us from unscrupulous and damaging behavior. With this tool, our consumers will be able to access all of their private account information and all public information that could be obtained by visiting our stores. The website has been designed with these two tenets in mind: simplicity (the customer can find anything on the site within three clicks) and functionality (the site offers the services that the customer is trying to obtain). It has been designed to empower our customers with information that will enhance the buying experience. The specific functions available are the following: online ordering / status updates on orders, personal account balances, electronic payment functionality, online product descriptions of our current inventory, product cost search in the local area to inform consumers where they can get the best value, customer feedback mechanism, E-mail Alert Service. We will offer direct mailings to customers who sign up for specific product updates and current cost savings. E-mail is a powerful marketing tool because it is driven by the very strength of the Internet—speed and convenience. It directs our customers directly to our website and retail outlets and allows them to make purchasing decisions in minutes. Customers desiring monthly payment simplicity can choose automatic withdrawal, and we will debit their accounts monthly on an agreed upon date. We will also partner with a 24/7 call center with access to our customers' detailed information to provide account information by telephone.

Tools Aimed at Enhancing Our Supplier Relationships

The strategy calls for implementing sophisticated electronic tools to enhance our supplier relationships. Improving these relationships will directly impact our goal of serving our clientele better than any of our competitors. Better supplier relationships result in faster delivery, lower costs passed on to our customers and enhanced products better suited to our customers' needs.

EDI Solutions - We are building an interface with our suppliers which allows us to use Electronic Data Interchange technology. This EDI solution allows our suppliers to see a live view of our inventory and replenish it to pre-specified levels. Our cost of carrying inventory is thus decreased while at the same time increasing the inventory selection for our customers.

Direct Order Fulfillment - For specialized orders, we have made agreements with several of our suppliers to send deliveries directly to

---

A Different View of Business Schools

As you are writing, you may wonder why leadership is such an important characteristic that business schools seek. Randy Giraldo, a student at Columbia's Business School has one explanation.

He says that business schools themselves have similarities to corporations. The dean is like a CEO who networks and raises funds for the school. The admission department is like the human resources department, recruiting the most talented students. And, the school's rankings are like their share price.

"The school needs to maintain a certain standard in order to maintain or improve their ranking," says Randy. Because of this, he says schools want to admit students who will not only be successful but will also become leaders in their fields.

"This ensures a high quality of alumni and increases the prospects for lucrative endowments in the future," he says.

our customers where one of our technicians will be waiting to install the product (if installation expertise is required) on the customer's property.

Procurement-through-payables - This solution will enable us to order, receive goods and make payments in one seamless electronic transaction. It also simplifies our order and inventory tracking by making all of the important information available online, including status of requisitions, approvals, purchase receipts, remittance status and the complete history throughout the purchasing and payment process.

We believe that the tools described above will put us in an improved and favorable market position going forward. These tools present new ways of doing business that match our customers' priorities while making us a more successful and efficient company. The customer experience will thus be enhanced and accordingly we will continue to flourish in this competitive marketplace.

Anonymous
Rice University Jones Graduate School of Management

My most significant leadership experience is not the result of one incident, rather the aggregate of my SEAL instructor duties in San Diego. As a member of the training group I had the privilege to meet many interesting students who taught me much more than I could ever teach them.

During my first seven years as a SEAL operative my job was simple: prepare for war and become a proficient and skilled modern day warrior. My responsibilities included the care of myself and the other 15 members of my SEAL squad. After my goals were accomplished I began looking for other challenging opportunities and an avenue to advance my career. I applied to become a SEAL instructor and was accepted. My responsibilities widened at a fast pace, instead of a group of 16, now I would have the responsibility of as many as 90 at a time.

As a SEAL instructor the responsibilities are great and the challenges are many. Teach young SEAL candidates to have honor, courage and commitment. Pass on all the experience learned so that when the time comes, the future operative will have the knowledge and skill to complete the mission despite all costs. Teach patience and aggressiveness, confidence and humility. But most of all teach the future SEAL how to think for themselves in times of great mental pressure.

When I arrived at the SEAL training command I quickly learned that as an instructor the future of the Naval Special Forces is put into your hands. I was responsible for teaching young SEAL candidates skills that could eventually save their lives or possibly cost them their lives. I wondered how I could possibly teach a class of 60 students whose education level ranged from Harvard graduates to a GED. I followed a few guidelines that I set for myself during my three years at the SEAL training command, and I believe it is with these guidelines that my leadership has prospered.

I have witnessed many good people rise to high levels in their careers or personal lives only to give it all away because of dishonesty. If we cannot be honest with ourselves and those around us, the business we conduct either on the battle field or in the office will be marked with problems. I think working hard to achieve goals with honesty and integrity will allow a person to soar to new heights within an organization.

As an instructor in the SEAL teams there are often individuals that do not share the same ideas or values. These differences many times lead to conflict. When there is conflict, communication is at its lowest and the teaching process begins to fail. I have decided long ago to share my experiences and teach to the best of my ability regardless of my personal views of an individual. This attitude has allowed me to conduct myself professionally on daily basis when I am in view of students and as important, when I'm not in view.

I also believe very strongly that we should never underestimate our opponent or the task at hand and never overestimate our skills. This idea allows me to stay focused on the task before me, and I do not believe that there are very many occupations where a role model is important as it is in SEAL basic training. I think that a large part of leadership is helping others achieve their goals. I was happy to learn that using the principles that I thought were important to me had improved the instruction of the students. This was conveyed to me by my superiors in the form of many awards. I earned a reputation of a fair but stern instructor that allowed me to earn the respect of the students. This respect is important because I knew that the students were listening to what I had to say. My only hope is that now during the global crisis of our country my previous students will be able to make use of my instruction.

Geoffrey V. Arone
MIT Sloan School of Management

Four years ago, I co-founded a company, saw the development and sale of my idea and helped lead Data Advantage Group (DAG) to $4 million in revenues in just two years. Through this experience I have learned what makes a company successful and what keeps it afloat during tough times.

Before embarking on this entrepreneurial venture, I sought to develop my skills in strategy and marketing and became channels enablement manager at pre-IPO Informatica. My drive enabled me to become the youngest manager in the 200-person software company.

There, I assisted partners who were in the business of building data warehouses that consolidated massive data volumes for analysis. However, our clients demanded higher-level visibility. I urged Informatica to develop a new application but was informed that instead "wireless" was the strategy du jour. I eventually found it too difficult to ignore this enormous business opportunity. My desire to develop this higher-level visibility product overrode my desire for options and security in the newly-public darling that had fostered my foundational skills.

I took my ideas to a like-minded colleague, and we started our own firm, DAG. I applied what I had learned at Oracle and Informatica (the ability to identify a need, conceptualize a solution and turn that solution into software) and developed our software, MetaCenter. To fund startup costs and software development, we invested some of our own Informatica IPO money and built a related consulting practice.

In two years, we had the first release of our software, revenues over $4 million, 30 employees and software clients such as Fidelity Investments and Palm. Our deals averaged $50,000 and are getting progressively larger. We partnered with Business Objects and Informatica and received reviews from Gartner Group and Meta Group, all without any large-scale funding.

Whether running a small family business or closing deals for software that I designed and developed, I have always felt most engaged running my own enterprise. From childhood through high school, I helped my parents run a tailor shop. They spoke limited English and required my assistance with all aspects of the business, from customer service to bookkeeping. Through my formative experiences in sartorial entrepreneurism, I learned that leading my own enterprise gives me first, consistent challenges; second, creative satisfaction and third, interactions with others on a professional and personally gratifying level. When faced with security and success at Informatica after the IPO or creating an enterprise of my own, I found that what I fear most are limitations to fulfilling my dreams.

I have learned to recognize and compensate for my weaknesses, take advantage of my strengths and have fun in the process. While my successes inspire me to pursue positions of leadership, the failures along the way to these successes illustrate that there is still much for me to learn. Sloan will provide an optimal forum where my classmates and I can share our knowledge from outside and work together on what we learn as we strive to become tomorrow's leaders.

Allan Boomer
New York University Stern School of Business

The Leadership Associate Program at Merrill Lynch was designed to groom college graduates for middle-management positions with the firm within two years. At least that's what the recruitment brochure said. In my case, the program's experience was a baptism by fire. Let me explain.

Although two-year programs are not uncommon at Merrill Lynch, the Leadership Associate Program was the first of its kind in the operations and services area of the company. As one of the first individuals to participate, all eyes were on me. I was a guinea pig in a lion's den, full of seasoned managers who did not believe that strong management skills could be learned by a college kid in two years. Although the chips were stacked against me, I was exceedingly successful in each of my rotations and was promoted to manager before the end of the training period.

My first assignment was to shadow a middle manager within the Cash Management Account (CMA) department, with the primary goal of learning the business and the secondary goal of contributing to it. I stuck to that game plan for the first few weeks but quickly realized that I needed to leave my manager's shadow and cast one of my own.

One component of my learning assignment was to observe managers' meetings. At the time, the hot topic was a software package purchased from an external vendor, Carrekar Antinori. The CMA department spent over $500,000 to purchase Carrekar's software, which was supposed to profile each Merrill Lynch client's check-writing pattern and produce a fraud report for any check not fitting the profile. After three months, management was becoming skeptical about the expensive software because it appeared to be ineffective, producing $0 in fraud prevention. My manager was especially nervous because he was the main proponent of the program's initial purchase, arguing that it would pay for itself within 12 months. If results were not produced soon, he would be at risk for losing his job. Here was my chance to emerge from the shadows as a key contributor.

Upon my own probing process into the future of the software, I volunteered to clean up the process. I beckoned the challenge without a clue as to how I might alter it but still steadfast with the goal to take any necessary strides before the ship sunk.

Standing Out from the Pile

Before applying to business schools, Lyle B. Fogarty contacted one of the admission officers to ask a few questions. She gave him some advice and used the example of working at Arthur Anderson. What stuck Lyle about the conversation was that he never told her that he was a consultant. When he asked her how she could have known, she responded, "I just assumed since every other applicant here is one."

That's when Lyle realized that his background was uncomfortably similar to that of many other applicants. He knew he had to think of a way to make his application stand out. He decided that he would differentiate himself through his style of writing.

"I've always enjoyed writing. I've always been a storyteller. I thought it would be a disservice if I didn't make that come through in the essay," he says. In one of his essays Lyle wrote about his distaste for olives, which was certainly unique. He felt that by taking advantage of his creativity and writing style he stood out, helping him get accepted to Emory University's Goizueta Business School.

Writing an essay that stands out is especially important when you answer a question about what you bring to a school. When admission officers think about their entering class of students, they want individuals who can add something to their student body. This is your opportunity to tell them.

A recent graduate of the Kellogg School of Management at Northwestern, Colby Maher also realized that many of her fellow applicants shared similar backgrounds. She says, "As unique and special as we all are and like to think we are, the stories start to run together. All applicants have worked at brand-name companies, done something unique at that company, attended a top college and ran a marathon."

Her approach was to figure out how to personalize her essays. Colby recommends, "Show self-reflection and a broader understanding of your environment in your essays. Your essays should be very personal, creating an image of you as a person to the reviewer, rather than a litany of accomplishments and accolades."

In my early analysis, I found that the Carrekar software produced many false-positive results, checks that fit the risk profile but that were not fraudulent. On average, each daily report contained 1,400 checks, with only between 40 and 60 that were worth researching. I also discovered that the process used to research potential fraud items was ineffective. The system's logic would need to be enhanced to increase the probability of detecting true fraud and the research process required streamlining. At this point, I had all of the answers but was hindered by the fact that my background in marketing and finance had not adequately prepared me for such a highly technical task.

For the next five days, I forced my ascent through the information systems learning curve, reading the 250-plus-page Carrekar Antinori manual, as well as a 300-page book on Microsoft Access. After learning how to create and work with databases, I appended the three-months-worth of records the software had produced into a database and began to analyze it. I met with management and representatives from Carrekar to present my findings and devise a new strategy. We agreed on a new "high-risk profile" and Carrekar modified its program accordingly. The database that I created was used from that point forward as a central repository for housing the daily Carrekar output. To streamline the research process, I created database queries that further rank research items, wrote a Visual Basic macro that systematically communicates research requests to branch offices and taught a team of representatives how to maintain the process for the future. The end result was an optimized fraud detection system that appeared to be more effective. Would it actually work? Fraud detection dollars would be the true test.

Over the next 30 days, I anxiously waited for the incoming fraud money. Finally, it happened. More than a month into the new process, the first detection occurred in the form of three checks from one account, totaling $57,000. The checks appeared on the report because their serial numbers were out of order and their amounts were more than 50 percent greater than the average check amount drawn from that account—two scenarios that fit the new "high-risk profile." In the old environment, these checks might have gone unnoticed. Within three months, Carrekar had produced more than $300,000 in fraud savings. By year's end, the program had paid for itself, identifying fraud at a rate of nearly $1 million per year.

ESSAYS

Achievements

IT CAN BE VERY DIFFICULT TO WRITE ABOUT your life's crowning achievement in 20 words or less on business school application forms. Fortunately, some schools give you more space in the form of an essay question. Many ask about your most important achievement. Some want a work-related achievement, others want a personal achievement and some want both.

As you think about your life's accomplishments and decide which to write about for this essay question, also think about what your achievement says about you. What strength does it convey? By writing about a volunteer experience you can convey your passion for public service and your desire to be involved in the community. On the other hand, if you write about an athletic achievement, you may underscore the degree of your self-motivation. It's important to consider which strengths you would like to highlight through the achievements you select.

If the school doesn't specify whether you should write about a work-related or personal-related achievement, try to write about a work-related example, especially if you haven't written much about your work experience elsewhere. Business schools place the greatest emphasis on your work-related experience, and this is a good opportunity to demonstrate how you have excelled in your career. If you write about a non work-related experience, then be sure to demonstrate how the achievement has prepared you for business school, either directly or indirectly. You can write about a personal achievement such as learning how to swim, but emphasize the strength that you exhibited, perseverance or tackling a difficult situation. These are strengths that business school admission officers like to see since they will also be an asset at school.

Essays: Achievements

Armando De Casas
Marshall School at USC

The National Association of Music Merchants Show (NAMM) was near. NAMM is the premier trade show for the music industry. At LG Inc., a woodwind reeds manufacturer, this event usually signaled a time of jubilation. However, amid this elation was an underlying trepidation that our long-played strategy would not come to fruition.

That year our objective was to attract new business, primarily foreign business, since our domestic market share was the largest in the industry. Our strategy for appealing to the foreign markets called for large capital investment in our product development and marketing departments. Prominent musicians from all over the world were invited to play test our reeds in hopes of securing an endorsement. After months of rigorous testing, a variety of world-renowned musicians gave us their exclusive endorsement. Management celebrated. This occurrence had secured the integral part of our strategy. Now we could leverage the musicians' endorsement and market our products in anticipation of the NAMM Show. Everything had been running smoothly until we encountered the unexpected.

As part of its strategy, LG stressed quick lead times and guaranteed same day shipping, which necessitated a system of high inventories. The nature of reed production was complex. The precise specifications that reeds require make them difficult to mass-produce, and at that time we were running low in the most popular clarinet reed strengths. During that period, LG was producing at full clarinet capacity. And although we desperately needed to increase clarinet production, I feared that I had exhausted all options. Obtaining additional machines was an option, but the machines were not very versatile. The engineers said that the flexibility of the machines was limited. Surely, I thought, it would be impossible to modify them, much less modify them quickly enough to address our problem. Experimenting with change and taking a risk were my only hope.

I came up with an idea that I wanted tested. I gathered individuals from various departments to develop a way to overcome our problem. As part of the manufacturing process, the machines in preceding departments could run both clarinet and alto specifications. I wanted to know the feasibility of modifying an alto machine into the desired clarinet in my own department. Moreover, it would have to be an efficient conversion process because time was not on our side. I assembled a task force to compare the structure of the alto and clarinet machines. The team was composed of two engineers, two musicians from the quality control department, the quality manager, the machine shop foreman and me. I intentionally played devil's advocate to ensure that the group would take a fresh approach to our problem. It was imperative not to assume anything but to examine the situation at hand. It was soon determined that mechanical changes could be made without great labor. Quality control was brought in to check the newly modified machine and adjust it to their specifications.

While all of the modifications were taking place, I worked with the materials department to ensure that there would be sufficient material to run through the machines in the event that the changes were successful. I calculated the required labor hours together with the proposed additional capacity. To meet the demand, round the clock production for three weeks was required. My employees understood that pressing situations like this would arise from time to time, and that they would be expected to help the company during such trying times. I was successful in rounding up the required employees and created a production schedule in anticipation of the added capacity. Finally, we received word that quality control had approved set-ups of four additional machines. We went on to produce the necessary reeds for the show, but barely made it. In the end, our efforts proved to be successful.

Being a part of this team was truly rewarding. More importantly, playing a leadership role in such a pressurized situation was an invaluable experience. To solve this problem, many managerial skills were required, such as problem solving, quantitative and, most of all, people skills. All of these competencies are essential if one wants to be a successful manager. This situation provided first hand experience of the importance of pulling a team together to work on a common goal. The goal would have been impossible without the cooperation of many individuals. Fortunately, we had a collaborative environment that allowed us to overcome the clarinet reed shortage. The experience increased my confidence as a group leader as I learned to better trust my instincts and embrace trying situations. I look forward to building my strengths and acquiring new skills in my graduate studies to combat the issues prevalent in today's business climate.

José Chan
University of Rochester Simon Graduate School of Business Administration

My recent appointment as a bilingual mathematics teacher in the South Bronx by the New York City Board of Education underscores many of my triumphs. After an intense selection process, I was chosen because of my high academic achievement, leadership qualities and professional success. Out of a nationwide applicant pool of 3,300, I was one of 350 people selected to become a New York City Teaching Fellow. In addition, I was rewarded with a fully paid Master's degree. Education officials selected me as one of the city's most accomplished professionals to teach in an under-performing school because they felt that I could make a tangible difference in the classroom.

On December 21, four education officials observed my seventh grade mathematics class. I divided my class into six teams so that they could discuss and solve problems in groups. During class, I guided my students by asking them questions about the percent problems that I had assigned. They came up with innovative strategies to arrive at the final answer. At the end of class, the head of the state task force congratulated me on having taught an excellent lesson. I feel that his praise of my lesson reflects my talent as a teacher and may positively influence his assessment of our school.

I have made sacrifices and overcome difficulties to achieve my classroom success. Instead of walking to a quiet corporate office, I take two buses and a train to get to school everyday. I try not to think about the salary cut that I took or the time that I have taken off from my career. The first two months of teaching were eye opening because of the new classroom culture that I swiftly adapted to. In addition, there were adolescent kids all over the place, and I had to learn how to become an effective math teacher in record time. Though it has been challenging to juggle lesson planning, homework correction and homework for my Master's program, I have no regrets because my classroom is similar to a business.

As a teacher, I introduce new concepts and assess my students' progress. Preparation, creativity, communication, reflection and patience are critical to this process. However, I realize that whether I am teaching or managing a brand I must draw upon these same skills. In both instances, I need to continually strengthen the efficiency of my team and our product so that we can collectively achieve our goal. In addition, I must continually inspire my team to reach its fullest potential. The only difference is that in business my goal is to grow a profitable enterprise, whereas in teaching it is to foster life-long intellectual productivity.

My teaching experience will always stand out as one of my most substantial accomplishments. As an effective leader, I must create an interactive environment where individuals will grow intellectually and an atmosphere where novel ideas will arise. My leadership will ensure success whether in the offices of a luxury company or in the classroom of an underprivileged school.

Juan Carlos Loredo
Jones Graduate School of Management at Rice University

A graduate of the McCombs School of Business at the University of Texas at Austin, Juan Carlos wrote this essay for Jones, where he was also accepted.

Throughout high school and college, I was able to achieve a great deal. My most significant accomplishment, however, occurred early this year. Since graduating, I have worked for TruGreen LandCare, receiving three promotions over the last two years. The most important of these took place this past January when I was named branch manager of the company's $3.7 million Houston-West division. Thus, at the age of 24, I became their youngest branch manager in the country by 10 years. I view the changes I have made in my division over the last nine months as my greatest accomplishment.

When arriving at the branch, I soon realized that it was losing money, the staff was fragmented and our reputation in the market was on the line. I was able to reintegrate the group by replacing several lethargic, self-serving employees with energetic team players. As a group we set attainable yet challenging common goals in order to direct everyone to the same ends. I restructured the business by evaluating the profitability of each of our jobs. Those on which money was being lost were renegotiated to an acceptable margin or replaced with new clients. The result was a more positive revenue stream. Then, by directing attention to time on the job, direct labor was reduced from 50 percent to less than 30 percent. In an industry as labor intensive as ours, this also made a significant impact on the bottom line. Lastly, we refocused our goals to achieve increased client satisfaction, thus regaining their confidence.

As a result of these steps the branch has, in the last eight months, gone from a losing enterprise to one that is clearly in the black. I view this accomplishment as important because of what it taught me about myself. Specifically, I learned to use time efficiently, successfully handle leadership and multiple responsibilities, work cooperatively with others, value their input and hold true to the values around which I conduct my life, even in the rough and tumble of the business world.

Accomplishments Count More than Responsibilities

For essay questions about your most important achievements, business schools are not looking for job descriptions. You shouldn't detail what your role is as a consultant, sales manager or teacher. Instead, you should write about what you accomplished in your role.

"Schools are looking for accomplishments not responsibilities," says Peter Gasca, a student at Georgetown's McDonough School of Business.

Peter gives the example of a sales manager. He suggests that stating that you managed a sales team for a large corporation is assumed, so a better answer would be, "I have been working as the sales manager for XYZ Company for two years now. During this time I was responsible for implementing a regional sales incentive program that increased sales revenue by 25 percent and improved client retention by 50 percent."

Citing concrete examples helps the admission officers measure your accomplishments. They will understand not just what you did but how well you did it, which will help distinguish you from the other applicants who were also sales managers.

Ruben Sigala
Harvard Business School

During my first year as a consultant, I was assigned to a prominent project in New York. Upon receiving this assignment, I called my collegiate mentor to share with her my excitement. During this conversation, she mentioned that there was an individual within my firm from New York with whom she had wished to speak. He was the national director of diversity recruitment, and she had been advised that his position authorized corporate sponsorship of scholarship programs much like the one under her direction at the University of Kansas. As a first-generation college student, the mentorship I received through this organization was invaluable. Consequently, although tangential to my assignment, I was honored to offer to attempt to visit with this individual on my mentor's behalf. Eventually, I was allowed the opportunity to give a presentation regarding the scholarship program. This meeting began a series of events that ultimately led to our firm's corporate sponsorship of the scholarship organization. This relationship has been on-going for the past three years, and undoubtedly has been highly successful for all parties involved. Having utilized my professional resources to contribute to the advancement of a community endeavor of such personal priority has been the most rewarding experience of my professional career.

My relationship with my alma mater provided the circumstances for another accomplishment. Although my family has always been an invaluable source of guidance and spiritual support, they were unable to provide financial assistance for my education. I was able to sustain myself through college. However, my financial situation resulted in some fairly uncomfortable periods. Through this experience, I learned a great deal about being resourceful, prioritizing and maintaining focus on my personal objectives. My collegiate experience was exceptional, and it greatly influenced my youngest sister's decision to attend my alma mater. Her enrollment directly succeeded my graduation. As such, I have been able to provide financial assistance to her throughout her education. This summer, Mary will be the second individual in our family to have earned a college degree. Watching her mature and develop into a strong and independent woman through this experience has been its own reward.

Finally, my senior year in high school I was named a first team All-American baseball player by USA Today. This accomplishment represented the successful culmination of one of my most difficult trials. I suffered a severe arm injury that prohibited my athletic participation during my sophomore and junior years of high school. As a young man whose greatest passion was athletics, the mental anguish of this loss was greater than the physical pain of the injury. I underwent surgery and an extensive rehabilitation process to regain normal use of the arm. The rehabilitation process was arduous and painful, but it instilled a great resolve of persistence and resiliency. Eventually I regained the ability to actively pursue physical activity again. Baseball has been a passion of mine since I was a child. It has served as a backdrop to countless family and personal memories. Consequently, at the conclusion of my rehabilitation, I fully dedicated my energies to playing baseball a final time in an organized setting. This period was one of the most enjoyable of my life, and shockingly, it resulted in a national honor. The recognition I received through this honor was flattering, but the real achievement was much more subtle. This experience had made me a much more appreciative and confident individual, and it is this consequence that has resonated greatest.

Anonymous
Jones Graduate School of Management at Rice University
The topic was to write about your greatest accomplishment and disappointment.

As a member of the Navy SEAL teams, I have learned many valuable lessons through my experiences. These lessons led directly to who I am today. I have accomplished many things in my life. I have had heavy demands on my time, and I am very proud of earning my degree while working over 50 hours a week. However, I consider the personal challenge of facing and overcoming two of my strongest fears my most important accomplishment. One lesson imprinted on my mind forever is that fear is a crippling emotion. In order to succeed in life's endeavors and especially in the SEAL teams, fear is a hurdle that until conquered is immobilizing.

Raised in North Houston, access to swimming pools or large bodies of water was infrequent. As an adolescent, I will never forget the neighborhood rope swing strategically placed beside a creek that ran through the back of my neighborhood. At that time, the extent of my swimming ability comprised only of the dog paddle and my aquatic experience consisted of swimming back to the side of that creek so I could get on the swing again. I never realized my fear of water until I joined the Navy. When I arrived at SEAL boot camp, I quickly recognized my inability to pass the swimming objectives of the SEAL training course.

One morning at SEAL boot camp the instructors singled me out of the group of students. The trainers thought I was faking my inability to swim in order to escape a 4:30 a.m., 60-degree pool training session. The instructors had a devious plan. They tied my hands behind my back and bound my feet together. As the instructors threw me in the pool, I overheard a trainer say in amusement, "Now let's see if he is bluffing." With extreme fear of my tight situation, I panicked and blacked out underwater only to awaken on the pool's deck. A doctor made sure I was physically well. Retied, the instructors threw me back into the pool. I blacked out again. The fear of the water overwhelmed me. The mental pressure was too much for me to control and my lack of maturity appeared. I'll never know if I blacked out because of panic or the lack of oxygen. At the end of that day, I vowed never to experience that helpless feeling again while in the water.

The next weekend I found a swimming pool in an apartment complex. I trained myself to avoid panic in the water and soon swimming long distances with my hands and feet tied became second nature. However, my achievement to overcome my fear of water is not the end of the story. In order to graduate SEAL training, a student must swim non-stop

Being True to Yourself

In an attempt to impress business school admission officers, some students shower them with unnecessary platitudes while others exaggerate the importance of business school by making it sound like a life or death proposition. The reality is that admission officers hate to read essays that sound as if you are trying to write what you think they want to hear instead of what you really feel.

"In my opinion it is critical to be honest. Tell the school your career goals that come from your heart and not necessarily your mind," says Kathy Hines, a student at the Wharton School at the University of Pennsylvania.

To make sure that you stay honest, keep your essays focused on you and your accomplishments. In other words, write what you know.

"Draw upon your own life experiences to make your essay unique and expressive of yourself. This will make you stand out," says Lisa C. Olmos, a student at the Jones Graduate School of Management at Rice University.

Every person has unique, interesting and valuable experiences. To successfully share these in your essay, you must be true to yourself and write from your heart and at times ignore what's in your brain.

in the ocean a distance of seven miles. I progressed very fast during the six months of my training. Before graduation, I placed third out of 40 students in the long distance swim. You may wonder why a person who feared water would become a Navy SEAL, but the challenge captivated me and my mind was set, failure was never an option. My tenacity prevailed and most importantly, I would not quit.

SEAL stands for sea, air and land. After overcoming my fear of the sea, there was one challenge to conquer, the air. My fear of heights strengthened as an operational SEAL in South America. My SEAL team was assigned to parachute and land in a small clearing near the Amazon River in Peru. I found myself in the pure darkness of night at 17,000 feet, looking through the back of a large cargo plane. I can remember thinking to myself several times. Will I land in the clearing? Will my parachute work?

Why am I doing this? Then I jumped. All would go well until reaching 5,000 feet. Upon activating my parachute, many of its lines ripped when opening. My parachute failed. I fell 3,000 feet more until my second parachute activated. Despite my troubles, I landed in the clearing. That parachute incident occurred 10 years ago. I overcame my fear of the air. Presently, I have completed over 300 military parachute jumps with success and with a smile on my face, I would like to add no broken bones.

The close knit culture of the SEAL teams adds agony to my greatest disappointment. I was very disappointed because I failed in the eyes of my peers. In the Special Forces a mission is often put up for bid to the most qualified group of individuals. We found our SEAL team in competition with an Army Special Forces team. The mission objectives were given and the two groups planned the mission from start to finish. We had five days to plan and then each group gave their mission plan to the decision makers in the form of a presentation. After the presentation the mission was given to the most qualified and best prepared group.

During my first year in the SEAL teams I was in Panama as a communications expert. For this particular mission I was required to create the mission specific communication plans. This involved the coordination of many entities including our use of helicopters, planes and naval ships. The complexity of the planning required me to publicly present this small part of our seven-day mission. At this time in my life, I was overconfident and rarely gave presentations. I thought I had prepared but nothing prepared me to speak in front of numerous Navy admirals, Army generals and representatives from the CIA. I was introduced as the expert, and I stood in front of the crowd only to freeze. I eventually gave the mission specifics but the damage was done. The powers to be felt that the Army team was better prepared and our SEAL team lost our bid to go to war.

I was told that we did not lose because of my inability to speak in front of a crowd, but I felt embarrassed and most importantly I felt as though I failed in the eyes of my peers. I vowed I would never make the mistake of being overconfident and under prepared again. I practiced my presentation skills and eventually sought a follow-on assignment to the SEAL instructor school that would offer me three years of public speaking.

My personal record of accomplishment has demonstrated an ability to set and accomplish goals. I acknowledged my fears and overcame them. My disappointments have taught me humility. I understand now more than ever that confidence is a must, but overconfidence often results in failure. My history demonstrates a pattern of success and I believe behavioral patterns of the past are the predictors of behavior in the future. I have had a successful career and many of those accomplishments proudly, I list in my resume. However, my most valuable accomplishment is not really listed anywhere. The acquisition of the intangible attributes necessary to succeed in varied and challenging leadership roles has continuously earned me the respect of my peers. Peer respect is a great achievement in the SEAL teams and my former teammates would gladly operate in the jungles of South America with me again. I consider this intangible accomplishment a great accomplishment and my true measure of success.

Camilo Román Cepeda
Wharton School at the University of Pennsylvania

"If you think you can, or you think you can't—you will always be right." —Henry Ford.

Two and a half years ago I found myself halfway around the world in the company of strangers who comprised part of a joint venture team between Ford and Mazda. Having just begun my assignment in Hiroshima the week before, I got off the platform of the Mishima bullet train station with 11 of my other American colleagues as we embarked to climb one of the most recognized symbols of Japan - Mt. Fuji. Our goal was to ascend the dormant volcano at nightfall to witness the legendary sunrise over the cloud cover in the early hours of the morning. However, without a single person in our troupe who had scaled Fuji before, we knew that the experience would be rigorous despite our best preparations.

Based on the recommendation of those who had done this hike before, our original plan had us taking a taxi to the fifth station about two-thirds of the way up the mountain, leaving one-third of the mountain to climb. However, due to our late arrival at the base of the celebrated mountain, we suffered a tremendous setback and had to hike an additional 12 kilometers on foot just to reach the fifth station. We had a decision to make: climb to the summit to see the sunrise or concede to resting at the fifth station and attempting the hike the next morning. Although all 12 of us were in the same physical shape, only six of us played to win; we attempted the summit despite the extra distance.

The remaining six of us ascended just above the cloud cover by the time the horizon began to illuminate. The brilliance of the sun caused us to take pause; we succeeded in observing the beauty of the sun sailing just above the sea of clouds, silhouetting shadows on the peaks of other mountains that appeared as sails. Still, the summit awaited. Three of us, exhausted and seeking mercy, were content to see the sunrise and go home; however, I was determined to stand on the pinnacle of the Japanese icon.

I had nothing to prove to anyone, but myself; whether I reached the top or not would only matter to me. Certainly, it would have been easy to start back after observing the solar spectacle, but could I permit myself to give up? If I had stopped there, would I have woken up the next day and asked myself, "Could I have made it to the summit?" Those who did not believe they would reach the top easily confirmed their conviction; I held firm that the opposite would be true for me.

The intrepid three of us stopped at a rest station to get an expert assessment of how much climbing remained. I spoke with the Japanese host:

"We've been climbing 12 hours so far, but..."

"12 hours? What time did you start from the fifth station?" he asked while pointing his finger at the milestone halfway up the mountain trail on his map.

With my finger identifying the base of the mountain I responded, "We began here at 8 p.m." Incredulous, his eyes swelled, as he surveyed our weary state.

"Ganbatte-kudasai," (Stick it out) he encouraged us.

This exchange was pivotal. I realized that only seasoned hikers pursue the summit from the base; we had shattered the host's assumptions. We certainly were underdogs, but even after the host's pronouncement, we never accepted that we would not make it. Hours later, the final 30 meters were in plain view as well-placed monoliths formed a stairway to the plateau. Humbled by the peak's sheer altitude and the magnificence of the panorama, we stood silent and motionless. Flabbergasted by our achievement, we embraced - against adversity we had triumphed.

Even today, I reflect on what that June 28 meant to me. The excursion, which started out as a tourists' weekend hike, became a trial of personal integrity. Attitude may not move mountains, but it carried me to the top of one. The experience answered many questions about what I stood for, and it gave me insight into my perception of the world. The attitude engendered by the three of us who reached the summit was one of belief that we would make it. Those who did not espouse this spirit resigned to a self-fulfilling prophecy. Perseverance in the face of hardship was strong among those of us who succeeded.

Although not everyone shares the same goals, I find it disheartening to see people accept mediocrity or leave their potential unexplored. When approaching a goal that challenges me to suspend my disbelief of what is possible, I consider the attitude that carried me to the top of Fuji. Failure is acceptable, but only if I attempt to win. When a project is falling short of its targets, I often ask myself whether I am giving 100 percent effort or holding back. In the final analysis, I must be true to my beliefs, as my integrity is one of the few things in life over which I have complete control and responsibility.

Since the climb, I have encountered many personal and professional challenges whose success relied on a winning attitude. Three examples that come to mind each had in common the perception of an unachievable stretch goal. It was my job to change people's mindset by challenging their underlying assumptions.

1) Goal: Reduce sport utility vehicle fuel consumption by 25 percent without compromising safety, performance and cost. Skeptics said, "It cannot be done; after all, that is what we have been telling the press and the Environmental Protection Agency for many years." As the lead engineer of the performance and fuel economy team, I put together a seven-year plan that improves the fuel economy of our vehicle by 30 percent while also improving performance at the same cost. Using planned technologies that reduce parasitic energy losses between the engine and the tires, we will improve performance and fuel economy simultaneously while maintaining competitive cost.

2) Goal: Increase matriculation of M.I.T. students into engineering positions at Ford by 40 percent over the previous year. Alumni at Ford said: "M.I.T. graduates now want jobs in high growth technology sectors coupled with large salaries we cannot offer; we cannot attract but the few students who are from Michigan." Leading the M.I.T. recruiting team as co-chair, we developed a plan for relationship building with professors and students to identify candidates whose visceral interest in automobiles is a greater motivating factor than a stratospheric salary. We have doubled the number of job acceptances this year despite interviewing only two-thirds of last year's figure.

3) Goal: Deploy a new CAD (computer aided design) system in 16 months enabling Ford and Mazda to share engineering data. Other team leaders warned: "Teams have struggled to convert from the Ford legacy system in 24 months, let alone 16. Moreover, with a Mazda interface as an additional requirement, the conversion may take twice as long. Best of luck!" Establishing a cross-functional team between Ford and Mazda's CAD departments and leveraging part suppliers and other teams' lessons learned, we developed a work plan to complete the task in 14 months. Mazda's participation became a strength instead of a hindrance since Mazda supplied technical support for legacy data migration, a key enabler catalyzing our conversion to the new system.

These examples illustrate the power of a winning attitude and a willingness to persevere. The teams in which I make a contribution know that I am playing to win. In my limited career, I have encountered some people who live without regret. They are the ones who do not stop short of their goals. I anticipate the members of the Wharton Learning Team to exhibit the same philosophy. Certainly, there will be many more Fujis to overcome and in doing so, Henry Ford's words will continue to resonate.

Valerie R. Ramirez
Wharton School at the University of Pennsylvania

My greatest personal achievement was being chosen as the recipient of Columbia University's public service award, the Harvey Picker Award for Outstanding Public Service. This award meant a great deal to me as I was the first recipient ever to be recognized for efforts to improve the student programs at the School of International and Public Affairs (SIPA). I earned this honorary reward primarily for establishing a successful mentor program and creating a second year speaker series, as well as volunteering for other educational activities on campus.

Immediately after joining the Master of Public Administration (MPA) community at Columbia University, I wanted to become involved in enhancing the quality of its student programs. After researching many opportunities, I decided to run for the mentor committee co-chair in the student government, which had a history of initiating programs that were never fully implemented.

After winning the election, I wanted to accomplish two primary goals: 1) transform the mentor program from an initiative with little direction and participation to a thriving, effective program with wide participation from the students and administration, and 2) initiate a new program to improve the outreach to newly admitted students. During my first semester in the position, I developed a stay over program in which newly admitted students could reside with second year students while visiting the Columbia campus. I contacted each new student to offer advice and solicit feedback. After receiving a number of enthusiastic responses from students regarding the stay over program, I decided to also initiate significant improvements to the structure and organization of the mentor program.

To ensure the program's success, I started the mentor program before the new students arrived on campus. Prior to starting classes, I matched each incoming student with a second year mentor. During the first week of orientation, I coordinated a mentor luncheon to facilitate interaction between first and second year students. With over 150 students in attendance, the event gained the full support of our dean who later provided funding for mentor-related activities. Throughout the next year, the mentor committee became one of the most active student-run clubs on SIPA's campus. Bi-monthly social events and volunteer second year tutoring sessions created an atmosphere for increased interaction between the first and second year class. The dean praised the program for its effectiveness in bridging the barrier that traditionally existed between the first and second year class. As a result of our success in improving the mentor program, 10 students ran for the mentor committee chair position in the next election. I was honored that the success of the program had inspired other students to take an active role in improving the educational experience for incoming students.

During my final semester, I witnessed several of my friends and classmates in the first year class struggling with the recruiting process. After losing three of its five full-time staff members, our career services department was not prepared to adequately coordinate the fall recruiting process. Sensing an opportunity to create a meaningful student program, I contacted the director of our career services to suggest a second year speaker series. This speaker series would allow first year students to hear from second year students about effective ways to find internships and full-time job opportunities. I immediately sent an e-mail to the entire second year class inviting speakers for the upcoming series. Within one week, over 100 second year students responded to offer their assistance. I selected six students to serve as the main panelists and asked the remaining interested students to be individual advisors.

To raise awareness of the event, I visited first year core classes and passed out flyers to publicize the student run event. Because of this publicity and the lack of career service resources, over 50 percent of the first year class attended the speaker series. With the positive response, I coordinated and participated in three additional series over the next month. The second year speaker series not only benefited the first year class, but also alleviated some of the career services recruiting responsibilities. Today, the second year speaker series has become an annual event.

As a result of the meaningful and lasting change that I helped create in educational programs at Columbia, I have developed a deep sense of pride for my volunteer contributions at the school. More importantly, the fulfillment that I gained from shaping my community and developing meaningful relationships has led me to reevaluate my outlook on life. Now, more than ever, I understand my need to balance a demanding work schedule with my commitment to volunteer work. Satisfying my personal desires to contribute and develop a sense of community has become a much higher priority for me.

Today, I remain actively involved in several volunteer activities. Shortly after joining IBM Global Consulting Services, I accepted a lead role in developing two IBM sponsored projects that help teachers in the Manhattan school district integrate technology into their curriculum. I helped locate corporate funding and recruited several of my colleagues to serve as volunteer teachers. Also, I spend four nights a month teaching a variety of computer skills to parents and students at the Martin Luther Junior High School in Manhattan.

My experiences at SIPA helped shape me into the person that I am today. I have always enjoyed taking an active role in my community, but it

---

The Importance of Visiting

Leticia Pearman thinks that not visiting the Columbia Business School may have affected her admission prospects. Since she already lived in Manhattan, she didn't think it was absolutely necessary to visit the Columbia campus. Ultimately, she was waitlisted at the school.

"If you're really interested in the school, go visit even if it's on the other side of the globe," she now says. She was accepted at Northwestern's Kellogg School of Management, a school that she did visit.

Students say that it is crucial to visit schools so that you have the opportunity to meet current students, get their opinions about the school and see how they interact. By making these observations, you will demonstrate a strong interest in the school and pick up some valuable insights for essays that you write about why you want to attend.

Colby Maher, a recent graduate of Kellogg, says you should visit even though the airfare and hotel stays can be expensive. "It's minor when compared to the overall cost of the school and the time you'll spend at the school as a student and an alumnus."

In addition to researching for essay questions about why you want to attend the school, you will also be able to better determine if the school is a fit for you.

"At the end of the process, you want to make sure you're going to the school with the culture that you feel most comfortable in," says Remberto Del Real, a student at the University of Michigan Business School.

wasn't until my years at SIPA that I realized the positive effect that small yet consistent efforts can have on a community. This experience has inspired me to continue taking an active role in my community where I can help improve the quality of life for others while at the same time satisfy my intrinsic desire to contribute to my surroundings.

ESSAYS

Overcoming Obstacles

BUSINESS SCHOOL ADMISSION OFFICERS RECOGNIZE that not everything in your life is perfect. Mistakes happen. Challenges arise. Bad decisions are made. What they want to find out from you is how you handle these kinds of situations. Many schools ask about how you have overcome an obstacle, a mistake that you've made or a bad decision that you've experienced.

When you answer these kinds of questions, remember that what's more important than the situation itself is how you handled it and what this says about you. In other words, if you write about overcoming an obstacle, keep the emphasis on "overcoming" instead of on "obstacle."

You want to help the admission officers understand your actions or decisions. Share your thoughts so that they understand your motivations and why you were able to overcome a challenge or how you came to accept your mistake. This will give them insight into how you think and the way that you make decisions.

Also, explain what you got out of the situation. If you write about overcoming a challenge, describe the strength that you gained from your accomplishment and how you will continue to use this strength. If you made a poor decision, communicate what you learned and how you will apply the lesson in the future. Admission officers recognize that everyone has challenges and tough situations. What they want to see is how you handle them.

Essays: Overcoming Obstacles

Anonymous
Harvard Business School

Confident, enthusiastic, and aggressive were among the words that described me when I first entered the workforce. I had experience in solving many technical problems and in leading diverse teams.

My assignment as an operations engineer for a team of field operators and one supervisor, however, proved to be very disappointing. The supervisor had a command-and-control leadership style that made it difficult for me to execute ideas. Scarred by years of neglect, apathy and arrogance from previous engineers, the operators had little respect and trust remaining, even for the abilities that I, as a new employee, might provide to their team. One day, after a heated argument with the supervisor, I lost hope and found myself on the brink of resignation.

I decided, however, to try one last approach. First, I had a long discussion with the supervisor and focused on understanding his views. I realized that many of our conflicts stemmed from his perception that I wanted to undermine his authority. A similar conversation with the operators made me aware of the lingering effects of past experiences.

I decided to assume the role of a student. Rather than focusing on pushing forth my ideas, I spent countless hours with each individual listening and learning. This approach eliminated the perception that I considered myself superior and showed the team my genuine desire to contribute. Secondly, I focused on building credibility by delivering results. As my work improved the operation, my circle of influence expanded and eventually gained full acceptance. The incident taught me an important lesson: leadership is earned, not bestowed. I made the mistake of assuming that I could leverage my title and past achievements to be effective. The importance of communication and patience were also reinforced. Lack of dialogue among individuals breeds unnecessary tensions and erroneous assumptions. Building relationships with people is time-consuming, yet essential for long-term value.

Lyle B. Fogarty
Goizueta Business School at Emory University

The Greatest Challenge I Have Faced...

~~Training for and running the Chicago Marathon~~ – Cliché

~~Getting an A in Chemistry~~ – Pedestrian

~~Climbing the highest peak in Spain in late January~~ – No good

~~Holding two jobs in college~~ – Nothing special

~~Running with the Bulls~~ – They will just think I'm stupid

~~Working at a client trying to avert financial disaster~~ – Expected

~~Hiking the Inca Trail to Macchu Pichu~~ – Hard but sappy

The dreaded encounter with the olives – BINGO!

Ciudad Real, Spain, 11 years ago—If my worst nemesis were a food, it would be an olive. Its cronies would be mustard and pickles. Besides those, all other foods would be on my side of the eating experience. If this were an analogy on the SAT, "Olives would be to Lyle as Boss Hog is to the Dukes."

My disdain for the olive runs deep. I do not know when this adversarial relationship began, but I can tell you when it intensified. I had been in Spain on a high school exchange program a mere two months. My Spanish was rusty but I was eager to make friends. One of my classmates, Tomás, invited me to eat at his house the following Sunday. Since eating at a friend's house is not common in Spain (Spaniards typically meet at a local pub), the invitation was quite an honor. Tomás' mother asked me on the phone what I liked to eat. Strictly abiding by the Fogarty code of manners, I answered that I ate everything put in front of me. Knowing how Spanish mothers love to cook and leave you satisfied I also added, "But Doña Antonia, just so you know, I eat a lot!"

Looking forward to the Sunday feast, I anticipated a heaping serving of Paella or a delicious serving of migas, a typical dish of La Mancha. The meal started out harmless enough, with slices of savory Manchego cheese and Spanish wine. Doña Antonia then came with a piping hot dish, surely the main course. She served me first proclaiming that I was the first foreigner ever to eat in their house. I asked what it was we were eating. She proudly responded, "Olive casserole, made with olives freshly picked at the family farm." I felt my face crumple into an anguished look, quickly catching myself, before anyone noticed. In my head I heard my mother's voice saying, "You'd better eat it!" As Doña Antonia served everyone else, I pondered my options—No dog under the table; no way to stealthily pour it back into the pan. Refuse it? Unacceptable! The olives would have to go in.

I took the first bite, telling myself not to overreact. As I carefully bit down on the olive, the juice squirted out, instantaneously reaffirming my revulsion. It would be impossible to continue chewing this bite, much less the heaping portion she served me. At this point there really was only one way out—swallow whole—an uncomfortable, but successful strategy. As everyone conversed around the table, I was in intense concentration. I was in an olive swallowing zone. It required perseverance and most of all, discretion to tackle at least 25 olives. I was proud not to break Fogarty tradition. I was especially proud that I took on my kryptonite and won, albeit with a slightly aching stomach.

After the meal, as Doña Antonia was clearing the table, I suddenly noticed a quizzical look on her face as she picked up my dishes. She looked at me and asked, "Lyle, what happened to the pits?" Quickly glancing around the table, I immediately noticed that in front of everyone's dishes was a little plate with olive pits. Flustered I responded that the meal was so good I had not even noticed the pits!

The story has followed me for years. I returned to La Mancha this fall for Tomás' wedding. At the elegant reception I saw the menu for an eight course banquet. At my place, however, there was a special menu just for me. It read, "One heaping portion of olive casserole." Signed Doña Antonia.

Patrick J. McGinnis
Wharton School at the University of Pennsylvania

The tics began when I was in third grade. I don't know what triggered them, but one day I started to blink constantly and unnaturally. At first, my doctor believed that I was simply seeking attention. Although that was not my aim, it was an immediate consequence since I could not stop the uncontrollable movements that provoked constant jeers and misunderstanding. After a battery of testing, my doctor discovered that I suffered from Tourette's syndrome, finally providing an explanation for my condition.

It's difficult to explain how tics feel to a person who does not suffer from the disorder. A tic is an insatiable urge to twitch that can be neither

Life-Changing Obstacles Overcome

When you think about people who have overcome obstacles, you might envision someone who has beaten cancer, survived a plane crash or been stranded on a deserted island. When you have to write about a life-changing obstacle, you might be tempted to find something as close to a life or death struggle that you can remember. Now that childhood run-in with the neighbor's dog begins to take on the tone of a life or death struggle in the wild.

But this is not what admission officers are looking for. In fact, essays that take relatively unimportant incidents and try to build them up into a life-changing experience only look silly. Admission officers know that not everyone faces the same obstacles.

For you, a life-changing challenge may have been when you were fired from your first job. Or it may be the stress from when you had to manage your first employee. Neither of these is a life or death experience, but they are certainly obstacles that admission officers would like to know how you overcame.

"Some people came from really destitute backgrounds or had horrible illnesses. I've been blessed in many ways. I got A's in classes, and I didn't overcome cancer twice," says Lyle B. Fogarty, a student at Emory University's Goizueta Business School.

Still, despite his lack of suffering, Lyle found a challenge to write about—eating olives at a host mother's dinner to be polite. No death defying act to most people, to Lyle it was a major sacrifice but also one that illustrated his values. "Sometimes the best stories seem to define you," he says.

Of course, if you have faced a significant obstacle, you should not be ashamed to write about it either. Abdiel A. Santiago, a student at the Kellogg School at Northwestern, almost didn't write about a time that he faced homelessness while pursuing his education.

"I considered myself a relatively private person and felt that I should keep out any of my personal struggles because they would be too embarrassing," he says.

> After friends read his essay, they urged him to write more about the experience. Abdiel then realized that by sharing the obstacles he has faced he could help the admission officers understand his background and where he had come from.
>
> He says, "As leaders we will be challenged and face failure on a daily basis. Revealing how you have triumphed over your personal failures will give the admission committee a strong sense that you are a real person, a strong person with a strong character and mature enough to talk about things openly."

avoided nor suppressed. Whether it was blinking, shaking my head or jerking an arm, the tics continued no matter how fatigued I felt from the constant motion. Being such a visible disorder, tics had a strong impact on my life. I was under constant scrutiny from teachers, relatives and strangers, and always tried to control the symptoms when meeting someone new.

The disorder's highly visible symptoms forced a decision early in life: would I cower with embarrassment, or accept and even find something positive in the situation? I realized that I would have to choose how I would live with Tourette's. With the unending support of my family and a sense of humor, I compensated for my fears by pursuing my interest in music performance. As I grew comfortable appearing before audiences, I entered speaking competitions in high school to discuss the realities of Tourette's and to share my perspective with the very people who stared at me. I also mentored a student with Tourette's who faced the same challenges that I had learned to surmount.

Tourette's syndrome allowed me to learn important life lessons at an early age. Before I was 10 years old, I learned to draw from a sense of inner confidence and courage. I realized that my peers' stares were not something that I could control. It was unfair to blame them for feeling threatened by something they could not understand. I could gain acceptance, however, by helping those around me to understand the nature of the disorder. In sharing my experience, I developed a sense of inner confidence that I carry with me today.

Over the past 10 years, my tics have diminished in severity and go mostly unnoticed. I am now able to control most of the symptoms by getting plenty of rest, but they will always be there whether anyone else notices them or not. Tourette's Syndrome is an everyday part of my life; it cannot be changed, and I have learned to see it as an essential part of who I am. I now think of Tourette's with a sense of pride, since it has changed my life for the better. By overcoming the stigma of Tourette's,

I learned to draw on courage and conviction in all aspects of life, from speaking up at board meetings and immersing myself in foreign cultures, to standing by my personal and professional principles.

Allan Boomer
Stern School of Business at New York University

As a first-year participant in Merrill Lynch's management training program, I thought that I had acquired a great understanding of how to manage people. For over a year, I had shadowed a number of managers, noting their individual leadership styles and the effectiveness of those styles in different situations. I was trained extensively in such management topics as situational leadership, employee recognition strategies, leading and delegating, goal-setting and roles of a manager. However, when I was promoted to supervisor, I quickly learned that there are certain situations that all of the classes and shadowing experiences in the world could not prepare a person for. Within weeks of having direct reports, I found myself swimming in treacherous waters. I had to resolve a conflict between two employees, nurture another employee during a tough emotional ordeal and motivate several complacent employees. Then, just when I thought supervising couldn't get any tougher, I had to handle a tense race-related incident.

I was hired into my supervisory position within retirement plan services. The person who I reported to, "John," was a seasoned 20-plus-year veteran with the firm who had spent the majority of his career managing within the retirement plan organization. As a new supervisor, I gravitated toward John, and he soon became more than a manager, but also a mentor, friend and confidante. John had also managed the supervisor that I replaced, so he was familiar with the team of employees under me. In fact, when the end of the year arrived, John and I teamed up for performance reviews and offered individual feedback to the team. I wrote the reviews and conducted one-on-one sessions with each of my six employees while John followed-up by doing the same. This approach helped to ensure that the employees' full year's performance was accurately assessed, since I could only comment on their performance during the latter half of the year.

A week after the evaluations, I was conducting a routine meeting with a direct report, "Jane," when she unexpectedly broke into tears. I had dealt with employees crying in my office before, but this time was unique. Allegedly, John had made some inappropriate "off-the-record" comments during their performance review follow-up meeting. The remarks alluded that because of Jane's national origin and heavy accent, she would have a difficult time being promoted within the firm. As she shared this information with me, I thought of my view of John as an extraordinary person to whom I revered and trusted - someone who I thought embodied the very principles of Merrill Lynch. He was also my boss. Jane was so distraught over this jaded evaluation that she had come to our meeting prepared to quit.

I explained to Jane that knowledge, skill and ability was paramount in attaining success at Merrill and vowed to get to the bottom of the matter. I also reassured her that there was no evidence suggesting that her accent had made any impact on her ability to perform as an employee and urged her to reconsider her looming resignation. I had never heard anyone complain about not being able to understand her, nor had I ever

---

A Pop Quiz Interview

After a week of waiting for an admission decision at a top-ranked school, Abdiel A. Santiago decided to email an admission director he had met to ask about the status of his application. Five minutes later, he was shocked to receive a call from the admission director.

Since he was surprised by the call, Abdiel was not as prepared as he would like to have been. The director asked him questions about his leadership experience and how he would draw on his experience in business school.

"I was not expecting a call back and consequently was not as sharp in answering some of the basic questions she had for me," he says. "After I hung up, I felt awful. I had just blown an opportunity to sell myself."

He says that he learned that he must always be prepared for surprises and that applicants should practice answering the four questions that business schools typically ask, which are: Why do you want to attend our school? Why do you want an MBA? Why do you want the degree now? What do you have to offer the school?

Now a student at Northwestern's Kellogg School, Abdiel says, "You should always be ready to sell yourself."

had an issue; furthermore, there was no such evidence in her file. Jane was exemplary. If John had truly made these comments, he offered them with no factual basis.

For the rest of the day, I deliberated over a resolution. I owed it to Jane, the firm and myself to handle the situation promptly and fairly. I did not want to rush judgment and accuse John of being prejudiced, nor did I want to ignore his possible remarks. I subtracted emotion from the equation and looked at the situation objectively. I needed to talk to John.

The next day, John denied the remarks, declaring that his constructive criticism of Jane must have been misinterpreted. He refused to apologize and behaved as though he was offended with the notion of our discussion. I explained to him that Jane's perception of his comments was her reality. No matter what he thought he said, what mattered to Jane was what she heard and how it made her feel. I suggested that John offer some amend even if he did not feel that his comments were inappropriate. He stormed out of my office as I sunk into my chair with a feeling of defeat.

Later in the week, John realized that he needed to admit his wrongdoing. Evidently, I issued a topic that rendered a dent in his tough demeanor. I was especially pleased, as I was preparing to assist Jane in filing a complaint to human resources, but did not want the situation determined in that manner. I engineered a resolution meeting for the three of us, at which time we agreed not to escalate the event. Jane, satisfied with John's explanation, decided to keep her job. I later approached John about his mea culpa and thankfully, we each walked away with a fresh take on two very important subjects: communication and respect.

CHAPTER THIRTEEN

ESSAYS

Teamwork

BUSINESS IS NOT AN INDIVIDUAL SPORT. A successful business is a team effort and to be a successful business leader—which is what business schools are training—you need to know how to work in a team. This is why some schools specifically ask you about your experience being on a team and how you work with others.

When you are answering this question, you want to convey not only the fact that you can be a part of a team but also how you have been a part of successful teams in the past. Getting a team to function efficiently is not easy. Business schools want to know what strategies and approaches you have used or plan to use to make your teams at school and in business work.

If you can find examples of complex team interactions that you have experienced, you should share them in this essay. You should also analyze how you worked to keep the team functioning and even what pitfalls you had to avoid. You don't have to be the leader of the team either. Being a good team member is just as important since a single member can easily ruin a team. In business school you will often be working in a team both as a leader and as a contributing member. It's crucial that you are able to function well in a group environment.

Essays: Teamwork

Jeff Marquez
Anderson School at UCLA

My first year of college baseball changed my perspective on life. As a top prospect in California, I arrived at UCLA with high expectations. Our team was comprised of extremely talented athletes with impressive individual achievements, but we lacked a team concept. Initially, our egos clashed, fueling bitter competition. As a result, our season began with frustration, disappointment and losses. I failed to make the starting lineup and quickly gained a new, humbling perspective from the bench. Prior to this, I had been fixated with personal statistics in an effort to gain recognition from professional scouts and college coaches. But, having been relegated to the status of "role player," I became aware that our team's struggles began with our individualistic approach. My arrogance and immaturity was reflected in our starters. I realized then that in order to win, our personal motivations had to be redirected towards coming together as a team.

I was determined to institute change in an effort to salvage the year. In hindsight, I successfully altered the course of our season through solid action. I initiated voluntary weight training sessions at 6 a.m. and lengthy runs after practice each day. At first, nobody attended. Undeterred, I persevered. My coaches began to make consistent reference to my increased stamina, strength and agility at practice. It was then that I received support from our team leaders. One by one, the players followed and we began winning.

These workouts strengthened our spirits, enhanced our physical skills and most importantly, voluntarily molded us into a cohesive unit. We went on to win the Pac-6 championship that year, overcoming significant obstacles.

From this experience, I learned that defining the problem is often more difficult, yet ultimately more important, than solving it. In this case, the problem was not that we were losing. Rather, that our selfish motives were destroying the team's chemistry, which is integral to success. Through commitment and personal sacrifice, we properly addressed the problem. The changes in attitude and approach became contagious and our record clearly displayed the positive results of our labor. As a manager in the workplace, I now identify all aspects of even the seemingly smallest predicaments prior to implementing the proper course of action.

Additionally, I realized that I possess an innate ability to motivate people, regardless of rank, through hard work and determined action. It wasn't easy adjusting to my role as a bench player. Initially, I resented my coaches and our starting players. However, my new perspective and specific course of action allowed me to become a catalyst in creating a successful championship season. Since then, I have always looked for alternative ways to contribute in any team-oriented situation because I know that no matter my status or skill, I am an integral part of the whole.

Camilo Román Cepeda
Wharton School at the University of Pennsylvania

The essay topic was to write about a marketing class team assignment due the next day, how you would approach the deadline and your role on the team.

When approaching difficult situations that involve working with others to achieve a common goal, a close friend once advised me, "Always err on the side of people." I have internalized his point to strengthen interpersonal relationships rather than risk compromising them. In the situation described, I would strive to preserve the team synergy and cohesion, while focusing on the goal at hand. I step back from the immediate situation and consider that even after the 9 a.m. deadline passes, the people on my team will determine the success of future projects that will reflect on each of us individually. Oftentimes, teams lose sight of this, converting frustration into blame and performing subsequent damage control rather than developing a solution. In the process of solving our current impasse, we have to take great care to maintain respect for one another and to focus on leveraging our individual strengths. Consensus on decisions is rarely 100 percent or even 80 percent, but 100 percent commitment to an objective can be achieved with due respect and impartial treatment of individuals on a team.

During a senior design class, I was part of a 20-member product development team designing a battery powered water-submersible kickboard. Monday was the date of our prototype technical demonstration; the preceding Saturday night six of us responsible for the prototype demonstration convened in the fourth floor wood shop with one waterlogged kickboard needing repairs. In addition to being under tremendous pressure to execute quickly, we were handicapped by the absence of two team members who had also committed to Saturday night.

Stress made some of those present livid over the absence of the two other members. After we spent an hour determining how to prepare the prototype for Monday, I worked to preserve team harmony. Having unsuccessfully tried to contact the absentees by phone and email, I suggested that we concentrate on completing the highest priority actions and not waste energy arguing how to exact retribution on the absentees. Preserving team effectiveness required scrutinizing the tasks and reassessing roles and responsibilities. The key skill I exercised was building consensus around what needed to be done and garnering commitment to complete the tasks according to our prioritization. I also applied my listening skills to allow our most frustrated teammates to vent their anger; I helped them rationalize that we could still get the job done by alternate means. In this case, I contacted one of the members of our business presentation team to cover for the absentees. She agreed that switching roles with the absentees would be best for the team. My efforts enabled us to complete our task without sacrificing team unity.

I know that my efforts to preserve harmony in those tense times were highly valued by my teammates; my peer review was testament to this. We were effective at delivering our objectives not at the expense of the individuals on our team. Just like the Learning Team, our members were not selected; we had to introduce ourselves and collectively achieve the team objective. My approach to the hypothetical situation would focus the team on the deliverables at hand and would obtain the commitment to execute. Perhaps the impasse could be addressed by a similar redistribution of work based on the different strengths of our team. Considering that all the team members are genuinely capable (after all, they are Wharton students), the challenge is not to execute, but to treat everyone equitably and with due respect. Congruous with the notion of being a true Learning Team, I would further propose to examine the root cause of our predicament and take steps to address it for future projects. Throughout the process, we have to decouple the difficulty or problem from the individuals. This protects individual dignity while allowing the team to focus on the challenge.

Valerie R. Ramirez
Wharton School at the University of Pennsylvania

The essay topic was to write about a marketing class team assignment due the next day, how you would approach the deadline and your role on the team.

Before approaching this difficult challenge, I would first consider the unique issues confronting an academic learning team. Based on my discussions with Wharton students and my own experience on academic teams, these issues can be challenging even without the additional time pressure. The non-hierarchical nature of a learning team forces students to lead through persuasion rather than through position or rank. Team members may confront cultural differences that make communication and agreement more difficult. In addition to cultural differences, team members may have widely different expectations regarding grades. Team members may also face conflict between leveraging the team's existing skills and allowing students to attempt more individually challenging portions of the project. Also, in an environment where students have experienced significant success as leaders, members may be reluctant to follow the lead of other teammates. Although the preceding discussion outlines the difficulties associated with a learning team, these challenges can help students become better leaders and team members. Consideration of these issues will also help me better address my most likely response to this time pressure situation.

In addressing a team conflict, I would first analyze the group dynamics and the specific role the group was lacking. Depending on the situation, the team may need a leader, but in many cases the team may need a follower to coalesce around a leader who needs support from additional team members. In most cases, because of my organizational and project management skills, I have taken a leadership role on the team. Assuming the team needed me to accept a leadership role, I would first listen to each team member's concerns and then develop an overall plan to accomplish our goal. Since time pressure is a key component of the problem, I would develop a clear plan with specific completion times for each element of the project and spend more time attempting to ease tension within the group. Also, as the project leader, I would be conscious of my leadership method. During my work experience as an IBM consultant and a campaign manager, I have had the opportunity to use my position to change team behavior. In this case, however, I would need to use persuasion to convince people to complete their assigned tasks, while also ensuring my leadership position is not resented by individuals accustomed to taking a lead role.

In my prior leadership roles, I have created smaller, more manageable work teams who work well together and who complement the other team members' strengths. In creating the smaller sub-teams, I would consciously consider the tradeoff between leveraging the team's existing strengths—for example, putting an investment banker on a finance project—and the benefits of challenging people with projects in an unfamiliar area. The time constraint may force the team to consider the most expedient solution—asking team members to work on sections that are consistent with their own strengths. After creating smaller work teams, I would articulate a clear expectation for the final work product and then allow each independent team to develop a separate solution. In almost all of my prior leadership experiences, creating ownership over the final work product was critical. If an individual is given responsibility and the opportunity to complete a project without being micro-managed, the work product is usually much better than if the individual does not feel a sense of ownership over the final project.

As the team members approach completion of their section, I would encourage a final feedback session for all of the sub-teams. I firmly believe constant feedback is an important element in improving the final work product. After receiving the final work product from each of the teams, I would conduct a thorough peer review of the final product checking primarily for typos and other errors that would detract from the professional presentation of the case. After the case, I would support a feedback session to address the problems that may have created the initial difficulties with the project.

The preceding discussion highlights the ideal completion of the project. Clearly, with time pressure and the team already frustrated with the progress of the project, additional issues may be raised that make completion of the assignment more difficult. As I alluded to in the first paragraph, cultural differences and differing expectations regarding grades may become a serious point of contention within the team. In order to deal with these issues, I would encourage open and honest discussions between the team members in a relaxed environment. As long as expectations are established and agreed to prior to the completion of the project, the problems associated with these issues can be almost entirely eliminated.

In order to illustrate the role that I would accept in a learning team environment, I will present an example from my experience as campaign manager for Congressman Bill Baker. With four days remaining before our election, I received a call from our chief of staff informing me that Senator Bob Dole had agreed to hold a fundraiser for us the next morning. The timing of the fundraiser put our campaign staff in a very difficult logistical position. Typically, our campaign would need two weeks to coordinate an event of this magnitude.

I quickly assembled a team of campaign volunteers to discuss our exciting opportunity and difficult logistical situation. To implement this project, I needed the commitment of the volunteer team to work both diligently and professionally. After deliberating for 10 minutes, I invited each volunteer who committed to this project to join us for breakfast the next morning and personally meet Bob Dole. This incentive sparked enormous enthusiasm from the volunteer staff and over 75 percent committed to stay. I then selected five captains to divide the volunteer staff into five groups. Managing five people rather than 30 enabled me not only to monitor the overall coordination, but also to identify and optimize individual group strengths. I established ambitious yet attainable goals to ensure the timely completion of the required tasks. After managing the project and volunteer staff for 12 straight hours, I was able to complete an anticipated two-week project in one challenging and exciting day.

Through my diverse work experiences, I have come away with not only a strong belief in team projects, but also a window into the world of effective management decision-making. Group environments allow team members to gain a level of effectiveness and team camaraderie that is not possible with several individuals working separately. Wharton's commitment to management education with a shared group emphasis will enable me to build on my professional team leadership experiences. Applying the same passion and commitment as a campaign manager, I now seek to immerse myself in the Wharton management curriculum to become a more effective leader.

ESSAYS

A Day-In-Your-Life

WHAT BETTER WAY TO GET TO KNOW YOU than to follow you around for a day? While the thought of an admission officer shadowing your every move is not too appealing, some business schools allow you to share a day in your life in an essay.

While you want to provide an accurate picture of what a typical day is like, you also want to make sure you read between the lines and recognize what this day is telling the admission officers about your experience, character and background. Obviously, you don't want to share a Sunday where you vegged out and watched football.

Pick a day that contains some of your more important activities. While you need to cover a day in the essay, don't over generalize. You don't have to write about every minute, but you still want to give some specifics to make the essay real and give it an authentic flavor of your life. So go ahead and tell the admission officer what you ate for lunch.

Essays: A Day-In-Your-Life

Anonymous
Harvard Business School

A representative day typically embodies my most important values: health, family, personal development, career and contribution. Below is one possible scenario, drawing upon a recent week of mine.

Awaking early in the morning, I enjoy a healthy, nutritious breakfast made up of natural fruit and low-fat milk. I head off to my field office for another day of work. As I gaze out the window of my car, I reminisce on childhood memories and the journey that ultimately brought me here. As I enter my workplace, my colleagues ask me to churn out the designs for the new pumping units and first phase of the new drilling program. We research necessary technical data and complete the tasks before noon.

During my lunch hour, I eat a small meal and take a jog around nearby mountains as I prepare for an upcoming race. I then meet with my team to brainstorm strategies to improve interdepartmental communication. I successfully help solve internal conflict between two work groups by facilitating an exercise illustrating the importance of mutual respect and understanding.

After rushing home for a change of clothes, I stop by a high school awards banquet. I give an inspirational talk on the importance of having vision and a plan to realize that vision.

I telephone my mother and two sisters. My younger sister tells me about her new job as human resource assistant, my mother discusses her progress studying for the Graduate Equivalency Diploma (GED) and my older sister expresses her happiness for my niece's academic performance.

As I get ready for bed, I pick up several publications including *TIME* and *BusinessWeek* magazines. I read attentively to improve my understanding of business, leadership and current events. I close my eyes for prayer and meditation, thankful for the opportunity to live another day.

Patrick J. McGinnis
Harvard Business School

As an associate at JPMorgan Partners Latin America, I collaborate with entrepreneurs, managers and colleagues to redefine the business landscape in the region. By working alongside management teams to address the financial and operational needs of a number of companies in different stages of maturity, I identify opportunities and take action to support their development. Whether I am working from São Paulo, Buenos Aires or New York, I invest in and monitor companies throughout the region and seek to provide resources that will create leading businesses and lasting value.

Today, I spent the morning at the São Paulo office of Tesla, an e-solutions provider in our portfolio. I met with the CEO and controller to discuss the potential revenue impact of a newly developed product. We constructed a financial model portraying the new strategy's influence on Tesla's performance. After lunch, I joined some colleagues to tour a hospital seeking capital to strengthen its oncology and cardiology units. Based on my research of the market, I agreed that a strong management team could harness an opportunity to improve the quality of healthcare in Brazil. Perhaps the most memorable part of the afternoon was the heart catheterization we witnessed in the cardiac unit. Later, my teammates and I shared our impressions of the visit. While I was intrigued by the hospital's potential, we agreed that it would be difficult to expand the business from such a small platform.

At the end of the day, I touched base with a fellow board member of Hispanic Teleservices Corporation to explain my proposal for a new variable compensation plan that I felt would best align investor and management incentives. After work, I met some Brazilian friends at a restaurant to watch the evening's soccer match and support the Brazilian National Team's latest charge for the World Cup.

Anthony M. Fernandez
Harvard Business School

7:00 a.m. – 7:45 a.m.: Wake up and go for a four-mile run.

7:45 a.m. – 8:30 a.m.: Get ready for work, eat breakfast and drive to the office.

8:30 a.m. – 9:00 a.m.: Sit down at my desk to check my email, voicemail and the previous night's sports scores.

9:00 a.m. – 12:00 p.m.: Lead a collaborative session to design the software system that my company has been selected to implement. These sessions usually include project team members as well as client representatives. Depending on the specific design area I am assigned to lead, I will also meet one-on-one with appropriate client contacts to incorporate their ideas into the system design.

12:00 p.m. – 12:30 p.m.: Return to my desk to document the work completed during that morning's meetings and record any open issues that need to be addressed in the design.

The Admission Process is a Process

When she was applying to business schools, Linsey Herman put a moratorium on socializing from September to November. She spent the self-imposed exile preparing her applications, writing and rewriting them.

"You have to treat your applications like homework," says Linsey. The effort paid off. She was accepted to Northwestern's Kellogg School of Management.

It's important to remember that the admission process is, after all, a process. This means that the more effort you put in, the stronger your chances of getting accepted. Applications require evaluation of your accomplishments. Recommendation letters require finding the right people to write them and giving them plenty of time. For essays, you will need to write, edit and rewrite to craft the pieces that best reflect what your plans are and what you have to offer.

Fernando Maddock understands this and spent a lot of time on all of the pieces of the application. He says a lot of people worry about getting the right GMAT score or GPA, but there's more to getting admitted than that.

"I realized that there was no point in studying for the GMAT if I threw my essay together in a week," says Fernando, a recent graduate of the Tuck School of Business at Dartmouth. "It's a process. Not one thing will make or break your chances."

12:30 p.m. – 1:00 p.m.: Eat lunch. This is usually done at my desk, as I am catching up on emails and voicemails from that morning.

1:00 p.m. – 2:00 p.m.: Attend the project status meeting and report to upper management on progress of work, next steps and any potential issues and risks associated with the project.

2:00 p.m. – 4:00 p.m.: Work directly with the software programmers to ensure they understand the design that my team and the client have developed.

4:00 p.m. – 5:00 p.m.: Represent my project team in a meeting that includes the primary contacts from each area of the client's business that is involved in our project. This meeting is held to clarify system requirements and design specifications.

5:00 p.m. – 7:00 p.m.: Return to my desk to check emails/voicemails, complete my design work and take care of my administrative tasks (travel arrangements, expense reports, etc.). On Thursdays, I leave the client site early to catch my weekly flight back home.

7:00 p.m. – 8:00 p.m.: Leave work and head to the gym for a workout.

8:00 p.m. – 10:00 p.m.: Meet my project team for dinner at a nearby restaurant.

10:00 p.m. – 11:00 p.m.: Work on various non-professional activities. For example, I will review resumes for potential new hires, organize a social event for my project team or coordinate a community service event for my company.

11:00 p.m. – Midnight: Do some leisure reading, watch television or talk on the phone.

ESSAYS

Cross-Cultural Experiences

WE LIVE IN A GLOBAL BUSINESS ENVIRONMENT, which means being able to work in other countries and cultures is now more important than ever. When you get to business school you'll also meet students from around the world who represent a truly diverse cultural experience. It's important that you can function in this type of situation.

Business schools may ask you to write about a cross-cultural experience. Or you may decide to write about one when answering another essay question. In these essays you not only want to show how you have successfully functioned in such an environment but also what you have learned and how you will apply this to future professional interactions.

Essays: Cross-Cultural Experiences

Daniel Añorga Cook
Harvard Business School

Isolating a single cross-cultural experience is an interesting challenge in itself. I have been raised by my native Peruvian mother, with a family spread across many countries, including Argentina, Brazil, England, Germany, Italy, Spain, Sweden and Peru. My life has been defined by cross-cultural interaction and international travel.

As a high school senior I was selected as a Dwight D. Eisenhower Student Ambassador to Denmark, England, Russia and Finland. During college I studied abroad in five Chilean cities through The School for International Training (SIT).

As a two-time Fulbright Fellow, management consultant and executive, I have advised Chilean, Venezuelan, and Mexican governments, multinational corporations and development organizations on entrepreneurship and international development. Over the past 10 years, I have traveled to 30 countries and spent over four years living in Chile and Peru.

But even with this background, I was unprepared for what I would discover—and how much I would learn about myself and society—as I began a month-long homestay with an indigenous Mapuche family on the Isla Huapi, several hundred miles to the north of Antarctica. I was here as part of the fall semester of SIT and I was to have no contact with other students or the outside world for four weeks. As the bus dropped me off on Isla Huapi, I began an experience that was at once exhilarating, humbling, challenging and critical to my current understanding of human and cross-cultural interaction.

Isla Huapi is nearly 100 percent indigenous and one of the least developed areas in Latin America's Southern Cone, accessible only by a primitive ferry. Running water, electricity, public infrastructure and basic consumer goods are all non-existent. Nearly everything consumed on the island was gathered, grown or built locally with minimal external contact.

Whether or not the "Westernization" of the Mapuche is inevitable, justified or beneficial, my personal experiences with the Mapuche represented a major shift in my thinking about cultural exploration, understanding and communication. In those four weeks, I was challenged to rethink my preconceived notions, personal beliefs and prejudices about a so-called "primitive" culture.

Latin America has struggled with an acceptance of its own indigenous roots through self-defeating social jokes, material exploitation, legal manipulation, violence and other forms of disparagement. It is often assumed that the indigenous are comparatively less intelligent or genetically inferior than people in more advanced societies. There is an underlying belief that wide differences in technological and political organization among developed and developing societies are based on the innate ability of people within these societies. Prior to arriving in Isla Huapi, I shared in some of the subliminal assumptions prevailing about Latin America's indigenous communities.

I benefited greatly from the time I spent at Isla Huapi. The experience shattered many unfounded notions and catalyzed a rethinking of my basic beliefs on culture and the differences between societies. I held firmly to a few fundamental guiding principals that I have formed throughout my life:

- Be passionate about learning from and understanding other cultures:

Listen and ask questions first, communicate and share experiences, enjoy learning about people's histories, how they think, make decisions and view the world. Be tireless, objective, open and fresh in your pursuit of cultural knowledge. Through experiences at Huapi, this principle evolved my thinking about indigenous societies and all cross-cultural interaction.

- Stay flexible, the unexpected is around the corner:

Dealing in other cultures continuously presents new challenges. At Huapi, I delivered a calf, herded cattle, slept inches from a flea-infested dirt floor, ate marginally, helped with chores beginning at 6 a.m., retired shortly after dark each night and contracted a persistent stomach virus. Without flexibility I would not have lasted one day.

- Always maintain your sense of humor:

Humor is a common and shared human characteristic with the potential for forming strong bonds across cultures. It is an ally, tool and bridge between people of unique societies—don't forget to use it! At Huapi, I spent some of the finest hours laughing with my family at our differences, cultural mishaps and misunderstandings.

- Most importantly, have fun:

Learning about other cultures is among the most educational, enriching and rewarding experiences possible. Cross-cultural interaction represents an opportunity to learn more about yourself, the history of nations, societies and humankind, the differences and common values across cultures and the social forces that have created the world today. If you can't have fun with this, why travel?

These principles helped me learn valuable life lessons through my journey to the south of Chile.

I learned that historical, geographic and physical environments have essentially shaped modern societies and the differences between people and cultures. The Mapuche's lack of historical focus on advanced agriculture, technology and complex political organization is not attributed to their innate abilities or intelligence but rather to their actual environments and social needs. They are extremely intelligent in their own environments and by their own standards (i.e., displayed a deep knowledge of plants, animals, native land and high levels of inventiveness, efficiency and ingenuity in survival). After spending time with a society labeled as "primitive," it was very clear to me that genetic superiority has not created the power structures and interrelationships between societies in today's world.

I also learned that cultural understanding and compromise is never a zero-sum game. All cultures have their benefits and problems. While Western societies may enjoy benefits such as better medical care and longer life spans, we lack in other areas, such as social support from families and communal relationships. Regardless of the level of development, all cultures and societies have lessons to teach—and to learn.

Finally, I learned that people invariably enter any cross-cultural encounter full of preconceived ideas, values and perspectives that have been established through their own personal experiences and isolated social environments. Cross-cultural interaction will become frustrating, one-sided and ineffectual without questioning your own beliefs, battling past assumptions, considering new perspectives and becoming open to that which is foreign.

Patrick J. McGinnis
Wharton School at the University of Pennsylvania

When my hometown newspaper, the Sanford News, proclaimed that I was to spend my junior year in college as a Rotary Ambassador in the "Paris of South America," I was slightly embarrassed to admit that I knew nothing about Paris and little more about Buenos Aires. The world I did know, Sanford, Maine, Washington, DC, and the stretch of highway in between, provided limited context. Yet over the next year, as I lived in Buenos Aires and traveled throughout South America, I gained incredible insight into cultures that differed significantly from my own. Initially, I was not sure if I would be able to truly thrive in Argentine society. I faced significant cultural and language barriers in addition to the logistical challenges of living in a modern Latin America nation. As I began to understand the language and culture, however, I learned to transcend these obstacles, see myself as a citizen of the Americas, and better understand my surroundings and myself.

Most exchange students are provided with formalized study programs, a flock of instant American friends and neatly arranged travel and living arrangements. In contrast, as a Rotary Ambassadorial Scholar, I was expected to eschew such conveniences and find my own entrée into Argentine society. I was chosen for this honor after a lengthy process that included extensive personal interviews designed to choose the scholar from my district from a field of 10 candidates. As a result, I took a leave

---

Stressing Out from Online Forums

When Juan Uribe first looked at the online forums for business school applicants at the BusinessWeek website (www.business-week.com), he found some useful advice from students who had been through the admission process before. But he also found a mass of people blowing the process out of proportion.

"I was already stressed myself, but the forums only fostered more stress," says Juan, now a student at Harvard Business School.

Applicants asked others who were admitted to give detailed information about their academic performance, GMAT scores and work experience to size up their own chances of getting in. When students began to receive their acceptance letters, some online posters asked them for their UPS tracking numbers so they could see if numbers close to them meant that packages were coming to their mailboxes. This seemed way over the top to Juan.

Stanford Graduate School of Business student Paul Todgham had a similar experience with online forums. He says that forums have some benefits but made many applicants overstressed about the process. He says, "It can have a negative impact on you. Separating the good information from the bad and resisting the temptation to generalize or group think can be tough."

While some students find online forums useful, most feel that you need to constantly separate the kernels of good information from the hype. If you find that forums only raise your blood pressure, then it's probably better to just avoid them all together.

of absence from Georgetown and directly matriculated at the Universidad Torcuato di Tella, a university whose demanding Spanish-language curriculum had compromised its popularity with most exchange students.

In order to truly experience Buenos Aires, I resolved to devote all of my energies to mastering the Spanish language. Learning Spanish was never enough, however, as my goal was to experience complete cultural immersion. I resolved to devote all of my energies to integrating into local society and spent the first few months observing my surroundings in detail and building a network of friends who introduced me to the intricacies of Argentine culture. After approximately six months of stumbling through sentences and translating in my head, I realized that I had become an adept Spanish speaker. With the trials of language behind me, I was amazed at how quickly I developed from the obvious foreigner to a fully functioning member of society. I joined clubs, sports teams and community organizations, anything that would help me to learn about life in Buenos Aires. By the end of the year, my friend Octavio, who had once been kind enough to discourage me from wearing a baseball cap to class, was coaching me on the finer points of argentinismo.

In the final months of my stay, I fulfilled an essential component of the scholarship program. The Rotary Foundation requires its scholars to attend five Rotary meetings as a guest speaker. These engagements allowed me to reflect on my experiences and share my impressions of Argentina. Through this introspection, I fully grasped the magnitude of the personal growth I had achieved. Although I initially viewed the engagements as an obligation, I enjoyed sharing my experience and ultimately spoke at 15 clubs in settings ranging from exclusive social clubs to modest neighborhood restaurants.

I am grateful for the time I spent in Argentina because it taught me that I could be an active participant in a society that differed significantly from my own. Although I was a kid from a small town in Maine, I looked for every opportunity to deepen my understanding of Argentina and gain a global perspective. I was able to integrate into the local culture because I constantly observed my surroundings and worked to become sensitive to local culture and customs. Although I was always willing to share my perspective as a foreigner with my Argentine hosts, I also strived to be seen as a resident of their city and a contributor to their society. When I returned to the United States, I realized that I now saw the world in a different light. During my stay, I gained an entirely new perspective on my own culture, encompassing everything from Argentina's reactions to United States foreign policy to the unintended cultural messages sent by some American movies. I immensely value this perspective and continue to look for other opportunities to deepen my understanding of the world outside the United States.

Four years ago, I returned to Argentina to work in Chase's Buenos Aires office. Although I had not been back for nearly two years, I was struck by the relative ease with which I readjusted to my surroundings. Still, significant time had passed since I left, and the country had changed more than I had anticipated. Despite my efforts to follow political and economic developments from afar, I had much ground to cover. Argentina was now entering a period of economic uncertainty that would eventually yield to a severe recession, political unrest and the fall of the government. I discovered that Octavio and a number of my other classmates were struggling to find work and contemplating moving to the United States or Europe. For the first time, I sensed a tension between my belief that I had truly immersed myself in the local culture and the reality that I was, in effect, sheltered from the challenges facing the country. Each time that I have visited Argentina since my initial return, I have been reminded that cross-cultural understanding cannot remain static. Argentina had evolved during my absence, and I needed to recognize and respect these changes.

During my time in Argentina as a Rotary Scholar, I developed the basic tools to effectively communicate across cultures. I have since discovered that the same skills that defined my experience are transferable as I explore other nations and societies. I frequently draw upon these lessons and recognize that my time in Argentina marks the beginning of what I am certain will be a lifelong connection to Latin America.

ESSAYS

Extracurricular Activities

YOU MIGHT WONDER WHY BUSINESS SCHOOLS want to know what you do outside of work in extracurricular activities. Part of the answer is that business schools want to create a class of students with diverse talents and backgrounds. By learning about your interests, the business schools can see how you fit into their mix of students.

In addition, however, you can demonstrate leadership or a strength that is not apparent in a working situation. You may also have a talent or interest in something that is not easily reflected on your resume like snowboarding or stock trading. Your extracurricular activities give the admission officers another view of you.

When writing about an extracurricular activity, keep in mind that you should not just describe the activity but also explain why you enjoy it and what you gain from the experience. Whether you've learned perseverance from running marathons or patience from woodworking, you need to analyze how you've developed through your activity. Learning about your activities helps the business schools complete their picture of you and your priorities.

Essays: Extracurricular Activities

Linsey L. Herman
Kellogg School at Northwestern University

The topic was to complete this sentence: "Outside of work I enjoy…"

…Hitting other people with rattan sticks in a Filipino martial art called Doce Pares escrima. For two years now I have been learning martial arts and training three to five times a week. At first I took it up to get into shape, but it's become my most fulfilling and satisfying (and time-consuming) after-work activity. Martial arts training has not only improved my physical conditioning but also changed my self-perception and my outlook. I work harder now on the mat and off, with more focus, determination, and confidence. In the process I have earned my brown belt and become an assistant instructor.

When I began my martial arts training I had to overcome an intense fear of failure. I was reluctant to speak or perform in front of an audience. My instructor recognized this, however, and repeatedly made me an example, both good and bad, for the class to watch. At first I was humiliated, then I realized I no longer felt self-conscious and that I was learning from his feedback. Likewise, I was afraid to compete in sparring because I had a tremendous fear of losing. My first time out in the ring I was beaten by a 16-year-old boy and then a 43-year-old mother of two. As I became a better martial artist—and discovered my competitive side—I began winning my matches. What I had to do, I learned, was set goals and commit myself to the discipline and hard work needed to achieve them.

As an assistant instructor, that's the most important thing I teach the children and adults who are my students at the studio: to bring out in them what I've brought out in myself. I push my students to set goals that as white belts they can't even imagine reaching. I know they can; getting my students to share my vision is another one of my own goals. Watching them slowly master the skills I've taught them is a different kind of victory.

Different Editors for Different Stages

Finding someone to look at your essays is critical. Whether you ask an employer, a business school student or your mom, it's important that you choose the right kind of editor depending on the different stages of your writing.

Paul Todgham, who attends Stanford's Graduate School of Business, had three types of editors. First, he found people he knew well to bounce ideas off them. They helped him identify which aspects of his life and experience were the best to present. These editors were helpful in the early stages of his essay writing when he was exploring various topics and trying to find which one would represent him the best.

Second, he found both current and past business school students. These editors had gone through the process before and often knew the unique traits of the schools Paul was applying to. They helped to focus his essays and make sure that he was matching his skills with the strengths of each school.

The third type of editor that he found was strong writers. Whether or not they knew about business school didn't matter. What was important was that they were good writers and could help him with his prose and, of course, catch any technical errors in his writing.

While Paul suggests this progression of editors to create the strongest essays possible, he also warns about getting too much editing help.

"You need to know your story, what you want to talk about and have a good sense of your content before you get feedback. Otherwise you start trying to fit yourself in a mold that was made for someone else," he says.

Jamil Ghani, who attends the Harvard Business School, also had a number of editors including a colleague from the consulting firm where he worked and a Ph.D. candidate. In addition, he says that it was important to get feedback from non-business school editors.

"Non-business school affiliated people are great for commenting on whether something sounds impressive or pompous," he says. He stresses that the essays should be understandable and approachable by all readers.

For Lyle B. Fogarty, a student at Emory University's Goizueta Business School, his mom was the best critic. She read his drafts and said that they were nice but weren't enough to get him in. Four drafts later, she gave her stamp of approval. He says, "You have to find people whose judgment you trust and who have an eye for what will work."

Regardless of who you get to edit your essays, make sure you get feedback from others before you submit them.

Anthony M. Fernandez
Kellogg School at Northwestern University

A student at the Harvard Business School, Anthony wrote this essay for Kellogg, where he was also accepted. The topic was to complete this sentence: "Outside of work I enjoy…"

It was a typical scorching-hot summer day in Georgia. The heat index must have been above 100 degrees. My friend and I had just finished making the lengthy uphill trek to the 18th green, and we were absolutely exhausted from the four hours spent chasing a little white ball around in the intense heat and humidity. The sweat made it look like we had just fallen into the greenside pond. We waited a few seconds to catch our breath and then finally holed out our putts to end the round. Whew! The suffering was finally over. No more than a few seconds later, my friend and I turned to each other simultaneously and said, "Let's play another nine!"

Outside of work I enjoy golf. I began playing golf when I was 12 years old, and I have been addicted to the game ever since. My love for the game has driven me to play golf competitively in both high school and college. To my wallet's chagrin, this love for golf continues to take me out to the course at least once a week. Aside from playing, I love just being around golf. I caddied at local golf courses during weekends and summers throughout school and just recently, I chose to spend a week of my vacation caddying in the U.S. Amateur Golf Championship in Atlanta. I also love to teach golf—it gives me the opportunity to take part in and promote others' enjoyment of the game.

Hello, my name is Anthony and I am a bona fide "Golf Addict." Evidence of my addiction can be seen through several examples like the one about my friend and me wanting to play another nine holes despite being ready to physically collapse. I have actually taken alternative commuting routes to avoid driving past golf courses on my way to the office. It bothers me that I cannot be out there playing. You can also identify my fixation with golf through my willingness to sacrifice sleep and wake up at the crack of dawn on a weekend to get out to the course. A 7 a.m. office meeting is unspeakable, but a 7 a.m. tee time is sheer bliss. What is it that makes this sport so addictive? Is it the camaraderie of spending time with fellow golfers, the enjoyment of being outdoors or the emotional ups and downs of the game? All of these factors contribute. To me, however, the main reason is that golf is one of the only sports in the world in which players of all skill levels can be as good or better than the pros at any given moment in time. I will never slam dunk a basketball like Michael Jordan or hit a homerun like Sammy Sosa, but I might sink the same 30-foot putt that Tiger Woods missed or hole out the same bunker shot that Jack Nicklaus hit over the green. These inevitable flashes of brilliance have drawn me so close to what I consider the world's greatest sport.

CHAPTER SEVENTEEN

ESSAYS

Most Valuable Possession

OUR POSSESSIONS SAY A LOT ABOUT who we are. They demonstrate what's important to us, how sentimental we are and how we make decisions. Business schools ask about your most valuable possession to gain this kind of insight.

Use this opportunity to be creative, to select an object that explains who you are. Perhaps your possession can bring up an accomplishment or experience that didn't fit in elsewhere. Or it can explain something that is meaningful to you that is not related to your work or career. Think of this essay as an additional opportunity to reveal something about yourself.

Essays: Most Valuable Possession

David Hall
Haas School of Business at the University of California at Berkeley

My most valued tangible possession is a second Great Britain tracksuit that was awarded for representing my country at the World Youth fencing championships 11 years ago. Qualification for the team was particularly challenging and required achieving a balance between the conflicting pressures of second year academic studies and international competition. By focusing my time, being flexible and setting interim goals, I achieved my concurrent aims of qualification and maintaining a high degree standard. The tracksuit therefore represents a major achievement in my life.

My most valued intangible possession is my ability to laugh. In difficult circumstances to be able to take a step back and find humor in adversity has helped others and me through difficult situations. It helps to recover perspective and refreshes the mind.

Anonymous
Haas School of Business at the University of California at Berkeley

My most valued intangible possession is my appreciation for my Chinese heritage. My cultural awareness has grown tremendously through the years. When I was very young, I was embarrassed of my Chinese middle name and felt that going to Chinese School was a chore. At 10, I easily preferred a McDonald's Big Mac over my mom's authentic Chinese cooking. However, as I grew older I began to appreciate the richness of the Chinese culture and found that there was a lot to discover and explore. I feel that growing up as an American Born Chinese has helped me open my mind to different people and experiences. I now take every opportunity to speak Chinese at home with relatives or when I travel to China or Taiwan. I also find myself exploring the joy and art of Chinese cooking and sharing it with friends. Most importantly, I find myself encouraging others, both Asians and non-Asians alike, to open their eyes to the Chinese culture and find something beautiful about it the way I have.

Recommendations: Ask for More than What You Need

You have control over how much time you spend writing your essays, how you format your resume and how many practice GMAT tests you take. What you don't have control over is how much effort your recommenders put into writing your letters, or even whether they write them at all.

Allan Boomer, a student at NYU's Stern School of Business, asked eight people to write recommendations, but only three actually followed through on their commitments.

"People are busy. They got tied up, and it just didn't happen. I didn't hold it against them, but it's a good thing I hedged my bets," he says.

Kathy Hines, a student at the Wharton School, says that as much time as she spent on her applications, she spent an equal if not more time working with her recommenders and making sure they were meeting their deadlines.

And while Linsey Herman gave her recommenders plenty of time and provided the support materials they needed to write the letters, she still had a problem with a former employer. She discovered that the former employer didn't spell-check the letter and while writing a complimentary letter, included points that didn't seem to fit with her goal of going to business school.

"If your recommender doesn't play nice, then you won't get in," she says. Fortunately, she also had other strong recommenders who supported her and she was accepted at Northwestern's Kellogg School.

CHAPTER EIGHTEEN

ESSAYS

Defining People and Moments

THERE ARE CERTAIN PEOPLE AND EVENTS that change your life. In various ways business schools will sometimes ask you to describe these people or events as a way to better understand why you are the way you are.

When you are writing about a person or event, you need to apply a lot of analysis. You want to explain how the person or event has had an impact on you and how you continue to be influenced even today. Show how you have been shaped, changed and influenced by these people and events.

For this essay, you can be a little more creative. You do not necessarily have to select an experience or person that is work- or career-related. Since the subject is more about your character and personality, the people and events will often be closer to you. They may have also taken place at a younger age. That's fine as long as you can connect the past experience to your present.

Essays: Defining People and Moments

Anonymous
Harvard Business School

Ten years ago during a graduation ceremony speech, I told my father in front of hundreds of townspeople something that I never before had the courage to say: "Thank you for your inspiration and example. I love you."

A month later—in a few seconds time—a semi and mid-size truck collided violently on Oregon's Interstate 97 freeway. When the sound of metal destruction came to a halt, five farmworkers were dead, two others were in critical condition and another-me-stood helplessly in the midst of the wreckage. When I walked to the driver's side of the truck, I witnessed one of the most horrific images I could have ever imagined: my father, gripping the steering wheel, head back and eyes closed. He was dead.

This event is one of the few that I consider a "defining moment," for it changed my perspective on life in many ways. The trauma of the accident and the pain of losing my father brought me a greater appreciation for life and the short time I have on this earth. It also made me realize that it is the difficult times—the times that bring tears, pain, disappointment, despair—that are the greatest opportunities to learn and build character. As I struggled and succeeded with appeasing my family's sorrow and faced the financial hardships that followed, my confidence in handling future obstacles increased tenfold.

Lastly, my father's death made me fully comprehend the many sacrifices he made for our family. Once an illegal alien working in unsafe and hazardous conditions and enduring many forms of racism and discrimination, my father lived his life in a way that his children could realize their full potential. In both my professional and personal life, I work diligently every day to honor his vision.

Daniel Añorga Cook
Harvard Business School

My character has been forged through 27 years of exposure to my most important role model: my native Peruvian, single mother has instilled in me the transcendent values of risk-taking, a global perspective, a disciplined work ethic and civic leadership.

At the age of 22, my mother took the ultimate risk. Defying Latin American social norms and her family's wishes, she self-financed a journey to the U.S., taught herself English and worked to put herself through college, rather than remaining in Lima to attend etiquette school.

After college graduation and two years of volunteer teaching in the destitute pueblos jovenes of Peru's Andes Mountains, she returned to the

---

An Email Snafu

We've all had the unfortunate experience of putting our foot into our mouths—realizing too late that the person who we are speaking badly about is actually within earshot. A similar incident happened to Harvard Business School student Dan Gertsacov, except in this case it wasn't what he said but something he wrote in an email that got him into trouble.

When Dan was applying to business schools, he was a part of a network of fellow applicant friends who shared their application materials to get feedback from each other. The admission officer at one highly-ranked school asked Dan by email to explain his quantitative skills. Dan replied to the admission officer and blind carbon copied his friends. Without thinking, one of his friends replied to everyone, including the admission officer, writing that Dan's response was good and that the business school didn't really know what it was doing anyway.

"My jaw dropped," says Dan.

Fortunately, the admission officer had a good sense of humor, laughed about it and said it wouldn't affect Dan's chances.

Dan's advice: "Don't blind carbon copy when you're commiserating with friends." You never know who will eventually see it.

U.S. Beginning as a juvenile delinquent officer in NYC's Spanish Harlem, she has invested 30 years of her life working to build up America's marginal inner city schools.

My mother also has an unflagging work ethic. Alone, she has raised two sons, at times working three jobs and later combining work with study to receive her Masters, Sixth Year and Administrator's Certificate.

This incredible woman has taught me so much of who I am and is an inspiration in everything I do. I've inherited her Peruvian heritage and passion for international exploration and understanding. Her risk-taking spirit has taken a new form in my dedication to entrepreneurship and readiness to take the path less traveled, such as choosing to join a non-profit startup rather than join the ranks of Wall Street. I've embraced her fierce work ethic, working 40 hours per week to help put myself through college. Finally, rather than deferring my social involvement for a future, undeclared date, I've made social leadership a priority in my professional and personal life, investing 2,000 hours in community service over the past nine years.

I will never forget how fortunate I am to have such a strong role model. And I have no doubt that, like my mother, I will continue to challenge myself to reach my life goals.

Ruben Sigala
Harvard Business School

During my undergraduate collegiate experience, I participated in a scholarship program designed to assist minority students within the business school. Students in this program received financial assistance and continuous mentoring throughout their collegiate career. This program has a profound impact on the development of its students, and I have developed a deep admiration for the program's founder, Dr. Renate Mai-Dalton.

Many of the individuals within the group are first-generation college students. As such, many have a very limited understanding of the opportunities available in a collegiate environment. However, through Dr. Mai-Dalton's constant and tireless mentoring, these students consistently become a collection of the most savvy, sophisticated and accomplished students on campus. The hallmark of the program is the individual attention each student receives. Each student meets regularly with Dr. Mai-Dalton to review academic performance and to develop campus and career planning.

She calls students daily to ensure that they are prepared to meet their obligations, and the group as a whole meets monthly to attend cultural events within the community. To maintain this program, Dr. Mai-Dalton sacrifices more financially lucrative opportunities. However, she chooses to dedicate her energies to this program because of her confidence in the potential of her students.

Dr. Mai-Dalton's influence significantly expanded my personal and professional priorities. She cultivated a sense of community obligation that has extended to my professional ambitions. Considering the resources available within the fields I am pursuing, the potential contributions are limited only by my creativity and willingness to extend my priorities from the myopia of my own self-interest. The private sector does not exist in a vacuum separate from the public sector, and it will forever be my challenge to contest whether my success in one area is fully contributing to the betterment of the other.

Jeff Marquez
Anderson School at UCLA

I was born in Mountain View, California, just outside the city of San Francisco. I was blessed with two amazing parents from distinctly different backgrounds who have shaped the qualities that I possess today. While my strong will to succeed and dedication to my family are characteristics that I inherited from my father, my creative interests and compassion for humanity have resulted from my mother's and grandmother's influence. Together, they gave me a unique perspective on life.

My sister and I grew up with the freedom to focus on school, sports and extracurricular activities. My grandfather on my father's side, however, was not as fortunate. He was born into poverty in Mazatlán, Mexico and was forced to help support his family at a very young age. At the height of the Mexican Revolution, he and his family boarded a fishing boat bound for San Francisco with no money and little knowledge of the American culture. The only thing he knew for sure was that America would offer a better way of life for himself and his family.

I did not fully grasp the significance of this turning point in my family history until I visited his birthplace when I was 13. I was shocked to see mothers sifting through garbage and unclothed children begging for food. The air reeked of sewage and the pollution was unbearable. Prior to the trip, I had taken for granted the minor luxuries at home that are simply unobtainable in such an impoverished environment. I found a new appreciation for the advantages in my life that resulted from my grandfather's courage and his commitment to his family. I understood then that the concept of providing a better way of life for our offspring is inherent in my family and has been my primary motivation ever since.

My father has instilled in me his ancestors' drive by setting a powerful example. One of my most vivid memories as a child was watching him graduate with a bachelor's degree in engineering at the age of 40. I was inspired by his will to follow his passions, undeterred by the obstacles that stood in his path.

I have always utilized a similar work ethic in my life, regardless of whether I am in school, on the athletic field or at work. For example, despite having a slight form of dyslexia, I was the valedictorian of my high school and graduated cum laude from UCLA. I have had to work extremely hard to master the fundamental skills of reading and writing in order to achieve such lofty academic goals. By observing my father's actions and successes, I persevered and overcame my disability.

The qualities that I attribute to my father are complemented by my interest in the arts, which have been influenced by the women in my family.

Start Thinking then Start Writing

A recent graduate of Dartmouth's Tuck School of Business, Fernando Maddock was surprised to learn that he spent more time thinking about his application essays than writing them.

"The hardest part is making the decision of what to write about," says Fernando.

It may be difficult to write an essay about why you want to go to business school because you need to have the answer first. For many students, this means that you will spend long hours or even days thinking about what your goals are for the future and how business school fits into those plans.

Jamil Ghani, a Harvard Business School student, viewed the application process as a time for introspection. He believes that starting with the essay question is the wrong place to start. Instead, applicants should start by looking at themselves.

"I said to myself, 'If I can't make a real case for going, then I won't go.' I didn't want to go simply because I couldn't think of anything better to do next in my career," says Jamil.

My grandmother was not only a concert pianist at the age of 12 but also an established painter and writer well into her 70s. My mother and sister were professional dancers and performed at the San Francisco Theatre. Upon reflection, early exposure to their artistic expression inspired me to create new worlds on canvas at a very young age.

While my mother and sister inherited my grandmother's grace and beauty, I was blessed with her steady hand and vibrant imagination. When I was five years old, I began experimenting with watercolors. I spent considerable time in our garage attempting to recreate simple scenes from pictures or post cards. My family's consistent encouragement bestowed upon me a sense of achievement in my completed work and motivated me during times of frustration. My grandmother said that art was an imaginary world of my own that I could delve into and become lost in if I gave it a chance. These are some of the earliest teachings that I can remember and, even at a young age, I valued her lessons and trusted her wisdom. As I grew, so did my appreciation for art. To this day, I still paint in my free time. I have since graduated from watercolor and now find pleasure in my ability to create with oil on canvas.

My ability to express my emotions through art quickly evolved into a sense of compassion for humanity that I also share with the women in my family. I have always sympathized for those that are less fortunate, which is compounded by my appreciation for the advantages that I have had in my life. For this reason, I have tutored minority ESL students and participated in the Big Brother Program. Further, each Thanksgiving my mother, sister and I volunteer at the local homeless shelter. By volunteering in my community, I gain a feeling of satisfaction by touching the lives of others who have struggled beyond my recognition.

If there is one area of my background that I credit to the shared lessons from both sides of my family, it is my ability to excel athletically. My athletic prowess is a result of the combination of coordination and balance inherited from my mother and the extraordinary commitment and drive from my father. My involvement in competitive athletics began with gymnastics at six years old. In high school, I lettered in three sports and continued to excel at the college level where I played Division I baseball for UCLA. My success on the field fuels my ambitious nature and overall confidence in any competitive arena, including business. I owe this willingness to accept challenges physically and professionally to my parents' teachings, as distinctly different as they may have been.

Because of my grandfather's sacrifices, my future holds no boundaries. An MBA will open further opportunities that will maintain the common thread passed down to each subsequent Marquez generation, the willingness to battle all odds in order to make a better way of life for our offspring.

ESSAYS

Passions

THERE ARE AN INFINITE NUMBER of things that can be your passion. Whether you are passionate about an idea, a person or the Boston Red Sox, there is no wrong answer to this question. Business schools ask about your passion to understand what's important to you and why. This tells them a lot about your priorities.

As you answer this type of question, make sure that you do more than describe your passion. Explain why it is a passion and how it has affected your life. More important than your passion itself is its relationship to who you are.

Essays: Passions

David Hall
Haas School of Business at the University of
California at Berkeley

Trust is something I feel passionate about. Trust is at the heart of any relationship as it defines the degree of confidence that contributors have in each other. In my career, some of the biggest disappointments have stemmed from an erosion of trust while the greatest achievements have been based on developing trust with individuals. It is also very important outside of work and one of my greatest honors was to be asked to be a trustee for my friends' son on the day of his birth. In all my activities I try to develop mutual trust with others and while sometimes this can be compromised I strongly believe that it is fundamental to contented and successful living.

Anonymous
Haas School of Business at the University of
California at Berkeley

I feel extremely passionate about my family. My parents immigrated to the United States in their early 20s with very little money. They knew very few people in America and struggled with the language barrier. My father often took labor-intensive jobs at night, washing dishes or moving furniture, in order to save money while attaining his doctorate degree. My mother, who was my age at the time, took side jobs waitressing or baby-sitting. They lived very simply and faced a great deal of financial hardship for many years. Now, 30 years later, my parents have achieved financial stability and are able to enjoy what their hard work has brought them.

I am most amazed at how my parents, amidst their hardships, were able to provide for two daughters and instill in them a strong sense of work ethics, humility and compassion for others. These principles have molded me into the person I am today and continue to guide me through life. My parents were able to give me these gifts by building a very open relationship with me based on mutual trust and respect. I hope to have such a relationship with my children in the future.

Showing Your Passion Outside of Work

Paul Todgham wanted to show Stanford that he had more to offer the business school than his business skills. He looked at his essays as a group and thought about what his recommenders might say. Then, he thought about what else he could write about that would round out his portrayal to the admission officers. Paul immediately thought of the 14 summers he had spent at the same summer camp.

"Business school applications are largely about business, but it's important to differentiate yourself. Schools get a thousand management consultants applying. Talking about my interests outside of work helped to differentiate me," says Paul, who attends Stanford's Graduate School of Business.

Besides allowing you to differentiate yourself, essays about your extracurricular activities demonstrate that you have interests other than business. Much of the business school experience happens outside of the classroom, and you will draw on these experiences to enhance the student community.

Peter Gasca, a student at Georgetown's McDonough School of Business, says, "It is important for any school that you are not a closet-dwelling nomad with no social skills." In other words, business schools recognize that successful leaders do more than sit at a desk and read case studies. Your extracurricular activities demonstrate that you have other interests and have achieved a balance between work and play.

CHAPTER TWENTY

ESSAYS

The Optional Essay

JUST WHEN YOU THOUGHT THAT YOU'VE SHARED every accomplishment, experience and thought that you've ever had in your life, there comes one last question. The optional essay asks if there is anything else that you would like to share with the admission committee. It's tempting to skip over this optional question.

Don't be fooled. In most cases, you should answer this question. This question shows that you are willing to take that extra effort to get into the school. It allows you the opportunity to make one more impression. While you may share another strength, you can also use it to explain any gaps in your record.

When shouldn't you answer the optional question? The short answer is when you have nothing else of significance to say. But if you're a future business school student we would find that hard to believe!

Most applicants use the optional essay to delve into a strength or accomplishment that they were not able to address elsewhere in the application. Also, if you have a weakness such as less than perfect undergraduate grades or a gap in your employment, you can also use the optional essay to write about this. You don't want to make excuses for any blemishes in your record, but if you have legitimate reasons for them you should explain them. It is better for you to fill in the blanks than to let them assume the worst.

Use the fact that you can write about anything to be a little more creative. Your other essays are defined by the question, but the optional essay is where you can really take control and say whatever you want the school to know.

Essays: The Optional Essay

Anonymous
Harvard Business School

I have taken the liberty of enclosing something with this application that is very dear to me, a replica of a photograph of my family taken nearly 20 years ago. From left to right starting in the front row, the photo shows me, my younger sister, mother, father and older sister. The place is Oregon, where my family and I migrated every summer to work in the sweet cherry harvest.

Using all my might, I would carry the bucket shown from 4 a.m. to sundown. Each full bucket, which weighed approximately 30 pounds when filled, was worth $1.50. At the end of the day, my earnings were approximately $20, a seemingly large fortune to me at this age. Although I was very young, I learned quickly that the more buckets I filled the more money I took home. To fill more buckets required me to work harder and smarter. Since I wasn't very tall at the time, I focused on picking the low-hanging fruit and tried to find and acquire the trees with the best crop. I would frequently wake up earlier than most of the other workers as I attempted to work the best areas. At the end of the workday, I would make sure to record the number of buckets I completed (including fractions of a bucket). Each night I would review my progress and ask myself serious questions such as why the number of buckets made this week was lower than last week. Relying on my father and mother's expertise, I would devise strategies to counteract the downward trends and sustain the upward trends. My younger sister, who worked alongside me and competed for the same fruit, was just as ambitious and intense. I would focus on ways to intercept her strategy and outdo her in every aspect of the work. I reaped the benefits of my hard labor at the end of the summer when my parents allowed me to use my earnings to purchase school clothes and supplies.

I would like to make several points in relation to this story. Number one is that it was settings such as these where I gained my first true lessons in business. Alongside farm workers who had little or no formal education, I learned the value of money and how hard work and ambition related to success. The daily struggles associated with trying to make ends meet with my family were very valuable lessons in finance, management and accounting. Competitor evaluation and analysis, focus on high returns and relentless monitoring of progress and performance were among the strategies I employed in the situation described above and ones that I still use today in my career and personal life. This situation and many other similar ones form the cornerstone of my success as a student, professional and community servant, as well as provide a foundation for my desire to pursue an MBA from Harvard.

Secondly, reflecting on such experiences has ultimately made me realize my true calling in life. I chose engineering as a major because I enjoyed math and science in high school and college, and mostly because these subjects challenged my intellect much more than other subjects. Now that I have worked in engineering for over three years, I realized that, although I can perform at the level of most gifted experienced engineers in my company, this is not where my passion lies. The science and math-based curriculum I completed in college and my experiences as an engineer working in the private sector have given me a strong analytical and technical foundation, which I will undoubtedly apply to other facets of my life. I believe, however, that my calling in the world is not to design the best process for producing oil or the most efficient way of bringing energy to the world. Although each of these objectives is an important and worthy challenge, my destiny is to help unleash the leadership potential of others. Whether it be working with disadvantaged students or motivating a work team during a project, I feel my true talents lie in helping others achieve that which they would otherwise not be able achieve.

There is one final point I would like to stress to the admissions board as they consider my application. I consider my ability to take standardized tests as one of my weakest academic qualities. Although I have learned and mastered the necessary knowledge to excel, I have never been able to master the subtle strategies and skills needed to achieve on such tests. The Graduate Management Admission Test was no different. I realize that I will most likely be well below the test average of your applicant pool. I simply want to emphasize that I believe my undergraduate curriculum and my technical work experience as an engineer have given me the skills and background to effectively handle an MBA curriculum. My passion, work ethic and vision, derived in large part through experiences similar to the ones I had during my days as a cherry harvester, will supply the necessary raw materials to further ensure my success. One piece of evidence I offer to the board is my situation prior to commencing my undergraduate degree. When I entered the university, I had an SAT score approximately 13 percent below the average score. I was successful in obtaining an engineering degree, graduating with honors and in the top 10 percent of my class. I hope to have a similar story to share later regarding my MBA degree at HBS.

I thank you for reviewing my application and look forward to your consideration.

Kathy Hines
Wharton School at the University of Pennsylvania

When I was 20 years old, my daughter Lael was born. I returned to Bain and Company to a very supportive professional environment and stayed almost three years as a permanent, full-time associate consultant in the Dallas, followed by the London office. I was one of only a handful of women AC's with children at Bain and proved it is possible to successfully manage a career, even in challenging environments such as Bain, as a parent.

I once read a theory stating, "Women with children are fundamentally disadvantaged to men in the workplace because societal norms require women to pay more attention to personal and home lives than men." I proved that does not have to be the case.

I feel through this experience, I bring a unique perspective to the Wharton MBA Class. I am not less of a parent as a result of my career, and my career has not suffered as a result of my parenting. In fact, I was recently highlighted in three different UK business publications as an up and coming independent businesswoman (*Revolution, eBusiness* and *New Media Age* magazines). I hope to instill in my classmates an increased awareness of the possibility and benefits of balancing a professional career and a family.

David Hall
Haas School of Business at the University of California at Berkeley

Elsewhere in the application, little mention of my motivations to pursue an MBA at the Haas School specifically has been made. While I feel that the rest of my application provides a general background for my MBA motivations, there are a number of specific reasons why Berkeley is a particularly attractive school for me and I would like to take this opportunity to expand on these.

Firstly, the major attraction of Haas is its focus and investment in technological entrepreneurship and global leadership. The school is highly driven in this area and matches my long-term career aspirations both in terms of sector coverage and international aspiration.

Secondly, if I compare my profile from those published within the prospectus I find that I share many of the aims and ambitions of current students, most importantly the desire for innovation and experimentation.

I see an MBA course as the perfect platform for investigating new ideas in a risk-free environment, and I want to be exposed to other students with similar ambitions.

Thirdly, I have not mentioned a second entrepreneurial interest elsewhere. This focuses on the environment and developmental aid. My sister has been working for a not-for-profit organization in the Tanzanian rainforests for the past couple of years and has voiced frustrations on the level and quality of funding that is being drawn through the sector. Concurrently, environmental issues are pushing further toward the top of government agendas, and companies are likely to take more of an interest in environmental sponsorship. Creating a fund-raising, profit-making company that also works to maximize investors' return-on-investment would seem to be an ideal market opportunity to exploit and develop. This ties in directly with the school's Social Venture business plan competition and is definitely something that I want to be directly involved with.

Finally, I am seeking a flexible curriculum. I understand the areas that I need to work on and those that I am already familiar with. I have also exhibited the academic maturity that is required to formulate my own program during my Ph.D. Haas' technology-focused but adaptive course structure is therefore ideally suited to me.

Besides being drawn by world-class academics, the school's location in San Francisco is highly attractive. Besides a passion for skiing and golf and the access to both sports that its location provides, I have a number

---

How to Know When a School Doesn't Fit

Daniel Añorga Cook figured out that a school was not a fit for him while on vacation. In April, he was at Carneval in Salvador, Brazil, when an admission officer from a top tier business school called. She said that she loved the application but wanted him to retake the GMAT.

"After wrestling myself out of my hammock and shaking off my disbelief, I decided that this school just wasn't for me," he says, adding, "Different schools appreciate different aspects of an applicant."

Daniel is now a student at Harvard Business School, which he feels is the perfect match for him.

of old college friends and students from the International program that live in the city. I intend to make the most of the opportunities that living on the West Coast can offer allowing these broader influences to complement the high quality Berkeley experience.

Anthony M. Fernandez
Kellogg School at Northwestern University

A student at the Harvard Business School, Anthony wrote this for Kellogg, where he was also accepted.

I wish the Admissions Committee had asked me how I arrived at my decision to major in industrial engineering at Georgia Tech.

Operator: "Good afternoon. Schering-Plough Corporation."

Anthony: "Yes. Can you transfer me to the director of the industrial engineering department?"

Operator: "Please state your name and order of business."

Anthony: "My name is Anthony Fernandez, and I am a student at Roselle Park High School."

Operator: "The director of industrial engineering is Mr. Yates. Does he know who you are?"

Anthony: "Uhhh. Yeah!"

Operator: "OK, please hold."

Mr. Yates: "Mr. Yates speaking."

Anthony: "Hello, Mr. Yates. My name is Anthony Fernandez, and I am a senior at Roselle Park High School. I am considering majoring in industrial engineering in college, and I was wondering if I could ask you a few things about your job."

Mr. Yates: "What is your name again?"

Anthony: "Anthony Fernandez."

Mr. Yates: "And you want me to tell you about industrial engineering?"

Anthony: "Well, I have been doing some research on the field, and I wanted to talk to an experienced industrial engineer to see if it would be a good major for me to pursue in college. I called Schering-Plough because it is only a few blocks from my house."

Mr. Yates: "Oh, I see! I'd be happy to answer your questions, but I am about to go into a meeting. I think it's great that you are taking the initiative to find out more about I.E. this way. Tell ya' what, why don't we set up a time for you to come in and see what we do around here? I'll transfer you to my administrative assistant and you could set an appointment up for sometime after school."

Anthony: "Great! I'll see you then. Thanks a lot Mr. Yates!"

I first learned of the field of industrial engineering during the summer before my senior year of high school. I did some research on this interesting field but was still uncertain as to whether or not industrial engineering was the right major for me. This uncertainty caused me to make the abovementioned phone call to Schering-Plough, a major pharmaceutical manufacturing company located near my home.

The resulting visit to Schering-Plough was fantastic. Mr. Yates and his team first gave me a tour of the plant. Throughout this tour, the I.E. team pointed out specific examples of how they applied their knowledge to improve how Schering-Plough manufactured, packaged or distributed their pharmaceutical products. I took a liking to the creativity of the I.E. team's solutions and how they used technology to continually improve the company's operations. I then had the opportunity to meet individually with several members of the industrial engineering department, including Mr. Yates, to discuss how my personal interests and career goals fit into their profession. The results of these discussions, along with the rest of my experience at Schering-Plough that day, made me realize that industrial engineering was a background that would suit me well. This realization eventually drove my decision to apply to and attend Georgia Tech, the nation's top-ranked industrial engineering school.

I consider this experience to be a very bold and interesting way to have chosen an undergraduate major. This experience is also a great example of how just a little bit of initiative can go a long way. Who would have thought that the director of industrial engineering for a $10 billion company would dedicate the better part of his afternoon to explaining his career to a random high school student? To this day, I am extremely grateful for the time Mr. Yates and his team spent with me. They helped me select an undergraduate major that has provided a wonderful foundation for achieving my long-term career goals of an executive or entrepreneurial position within a product-driven manufacturing company. Lastly, I would be remiss if I did not thank Schering-Plough's phone operator for actually thinking that Mr. Yates knew who I was.

CHAPTER TWENTY-ONE

Finishing Touches

Finishing Touches

At this point you know everything that you need in order to write a successful essay. All that's left to do is you have to write it. As you are finishing your essays, we have a few suggestions to help ensure that it's a winner.

Finding Three Types of Editors

As writers have different styles so do editors. When you are showing your essay to editors you may find that your business colleagues edit your essays differently than your English professor. A business colleague may you give you feedback on the way that you convey your business skills while your English professor might focus on the essay's continuity and even word choice.

Because there are three things that you would like your editors to read for, there are three types of editors that you need. You don't necessarily need to find three different people since some are capable of doing more than one task.

The first editor that you need is someone like a business professor, colleague or business school student or graduate who can read your essays for their business importance. Ask them to note your preparation for an MBA, your line of reasoning for why you'd like the degree and the reflection of the skills that are needed for the program. Have them help you describe your strengths as a business leader and team member as well as analyze your accomplishments.

The second editor that you need is someone like an English professor or a writer who can comment on the actual writing in your essays. Do you describe your accomplishments in an interesting way? How is the flow of your thoughts? Can you enhance the description or narration? This second type of editor should analyze your writing style.

And, the third editor is a copy editor, someone who can check your spelling, grammar and punctuation. This editor will make sure that you have the right name of the school in your essays and free your work from typos.

While getting feedback will help you to refine your thoughts and polish your writing, you have to be careful to retain your own voice in your essays. Your editors should provide input but not rewrite your essays. You don't want your essays to sound like they were written by a committee of editors.

Recycling

Most business school admission officers warn against recycling. This is because they can tell when you are reusing an essay from one school for another. Often the essay that an applicant chooses to reuse does not specifically address the question posed by the school. Or it is a general answer that does not contain specific examples from the school. However, this does not mean that you cannot use parts of your essays that you wrote for other applications. The key is that you need to approach each essay as if it is the only one you are writing for the specific school. You will need to do some heavy editing and modifications. Don't get lazy and just copy and paste.

Always be sure that your recycled essays answer the specific question of the school. Also they should present the strengths needed for that school. You should not be able to detect that you have used the essay for another application.

Parting Words

When we asked business school admission officers why they like their job and what motivates them to get up each morning, many of them had the same reason. They enjoy seeing students who are at a crossroads in their life and who see their future enhanced by an MBA. They take great pleasure in helping students attain the degree and make their goals a reality.

When you think of admission officers this way, you realize that they are not looking at reasons to keep you out of business school but for reasons to admit you. They are on your side. Your job is to provide them with the reasons to let you in. Spend the time to think about your accomplishments, about your reasons for going to business school and how you will use the degree to succeed in the future. If you do this, you will create some thoughtful and memorable essays.

Some students think that they should build up their accomplishments or exaggerate a strength that they don't really have to gain admission. The reality is that admission officers are looking for the real you. And, believe it or not, the real you has something extraordinary to say.

Business School is More than an Education

When it comes to making the final decision about which school to attend, you will need to ask yourself some serious questions. Martin Morgades, a student at Rice's Jones Graduate School of Management, says you should ask why you want to attend a particular school and where you will be most comfortable.

"Don't just go to a 'name-brand' school just because others do," he advises.

After all, your choice of school will affect you long after you graduate. You will gain the tools you need to advance your career, maybe even change careers and make lasting friendships.

"Business school has been one of the most rewarding experiences of my life. Remember that these experiences are priceless, and you should have no reservations about your decision," says Peter Gasca, who attends Georgetown's McDonough School of Business.

Contributors and Organizations

Geoffrey V. Arone is a graduate of Brown University and attends the MIT Sloan School of Management. He is the co-founder of Data Advantage Group, a business intelligence software business that has generated over $5 million in revenue. He has also worked as a channels enablement manager at Informatica Corporation and product analyst at Oracle Corporation. Outside of work, he was the lead singer and keyboard player for an alternative rock band, Big Toy Fun and a member of Full Circle Fund, a Silicon Valley nonprofit organization. He plans to start a technology-related company after graduating.

Julie R. Barefoot is the assistant dean and director of MBA admissions at the Goizueta Business School at Emory University. She holds her MBA from the University of North Carolina at Chapel Hill (MBA '83). In addition to her duties at Goizueta, Julie is serving a three-year term as an elected board member to the Graduate Management Admissions Council (GMAC). She was also the first staff recipient of the Keough Award for Excellence at Goizueta Business School.

Allan Boomer is a graduate of Morgan State University and attends the New York University Stern School of Business on a full tuition merit-based scholarship. He founded his college's first on-campus barber shop and started an event management company while an undergraduate. After graduating, he participated in the Leadership Associate Program, a two-year management training program, at Merrill Lynch and became a Six Sigma Black Belt, a highly-trained statistician and project manager who led teams through efficiency initiatives. He plans to be an entrepreneur after graduating.

Camilo Román Cepeda is a graduate of MIT and a recent graduate of the Wharton School and the Lauder Institute of Management and International Studies at the University of Pennsylvania. He was a product engineer at Ford, where he worked in Hiroshima on the first Ford-Mazda joint engineering vehicle program. He has recently joined Samsung's global strategy group based in Seoul, where he is using his experiences from Wharton and Lauder to help globalize the company.

José Chan is a graduate of Cornell University and a recent graduate of the Simon Graduate School of Business Administration at the University of Rochester. Before business school, he had diverse experiences working part-time and full-time in the apparel industry in Europe, Asia and the Americas as well as teaching math in the Bronx. He plans to work in the luxury products sector.

Dan Cook is a graduate of Fairfield University and a student at the Harvard Business School. He has spent seven years working with high growth entrepreneurs in the U.S. and Latin America. Most recently, he was a vice president at Endeavor, a development organization that has raised approximately $500 million for entrepreneurs in Argentina, Brazil, Chile, Mexico and Uruguay. Prior to Endeavor, Dan was awarded the Fulbright Fellowship to analyze entrepreneurial finance in Chile. He was also one of the first five employees at Sagemaker, a software start-up that raised more than $30 million in venture capital from GE Equity, Enertech and Internet Capital Group. He is president of Harvard Business School's Sustainable Development Club and co-founder of a project to install the first solar energy modules at Harvard. He values community service, having volunteered more than 2,000 hours during the past 10 years.

Martin R. Curiel is a graduate of Cal Poly San Luis Obispo and a student at the Harvard Business School. Despite the doubts of friends and even teachers, he became the first in his family to graduate from college.

Armando De Casas is a graduate of Cal Poly Pomona and a recent graduate of the Marshall School of Business at USC. He was the first in his extended family to graduate from college and currently works as a senior financial analyst at a Fortune 500 company in Los Angeles.

Randall Dean is the former director of admission at the Michigan State University Broad Graduate School Of Management. He now works as a marketing strategist at Pace & Partners, a Michigan marketing communications firm.

Remberto Del Real is a graduate of the University of Illinois-Chicago and a recent graduate of the University of Michigan Business School, where he was a Consortium for Graduate Study in Management Fellow. Before business school, he worked in marketing at Ace Hardware Corporation. He enjoys stand-up comedy and is a former member of A Second City-Chicago improv troupe.

Richard A. Delgado is a graduate of Swarthmore College and a student at the Southern Methodist University Cox School of Business. He has worked as a marketing and commercial services associate and public affairs manager at the Columbia Energy Group. Outside of work, he is on the board of directors of Volunteer Fairfax and the CARMA Foundation.

Anthony M. Fernandez is a graduate of the Georgia Institute of Technology and a student at the Harvard Business School. He has worked as a management consultant at Cap Gemini Ernst & Young (CGE&Y) and in manufacturing at Ford Motor Company and Barré Company. While at CGE&Y, he was the firm's organizer of an Atlanta Community Service Day, where he coordinated and led a team that landscaped and painted a drug and alcohol rehabilitation center. He plans to work in product marketing or brand management after graduating.

Lyle B. Fogarty is a graduate of the University of Notre Dame and a recent graduate of Emory University's Goizueta Business School. He has worked as a senior consultant at Arthur Anderson and a commercial lender at SunTrust Bank. Post business school, he secured a job in the real estate development group at Trammell Crow Company. In addition to running the Chicago Marathon and climbing the highest peak in Spain, he has also run with the bulls.

Gabriel Freund is a graduate of the University of Puerto Rico and a student at the University of Michigan Business School. He worked on Wall Street in different positions for the "bulge bracket" investment banks and plans to return to the industry after graduating. He says, "I love where I am. I am getting a world-class education in one of the top 10 business schools in the world, and I'm a student again at almost 30 years old!"

Peter Gasca is a graduate of Arizona State University and a recent graduate of Georgetown's McDonough School of Business, where he conducted interviews for the MBA admission department. He plans to work in international real estate development and business strategy.

Dan Gertsacov is a graduate of the University of Richmond and a student at the Harvard Business School. He was formerly a Fulbright Fellow in Chile and founded Forum EMPRESA, a non-profit organization based in Brazil to promote corporate social responsibility in Latin America and the Caribbean. He has recently worked during the summer with MTV Latin America to help launch their first social awareness campaign. After graduating from HBS, Dan will focus on leveraging the power of media to make a positive difference in the world.

Jamil Ghani is a graduate of Harvard College and a student at Harvard Business School. He has worked as a management consultant at Boston Consulting Group, where he was promoted to the post-MBA position after only 18 months, and in Microsoft's corporate strategy group. An avid photographer, the Miami native is the first in his family to have attended college.

Randy Giraldo is a graduate of the Stevens Institute of Technology and a student at the Columbia Business School. He has worked as a project manager at Bovis Lend Lease, implementing a plan for the potential real estate development of the New York Passenger Ship Terminal and managing the project procurement of the Goldman Sachs Learning Center. He plans to pursue a career in the real estate finance industry after graduation.

David Hall received his undergraduate degree in aeronautical engineering and Ph.D. in combat aircraft design at Imperial College and is a student at Berkeley's Haas School of Business. He has worked in direct line management and as a freelance consultant and represented Britain in the World Youth fencing championships. After graduation, he plans to work as a high tech entrepreneur.

Linsey Herman is a graduate of Harvard College and a recent graduate of Northwestern's Kellogg School of Management. Before business school, she received a degree in culinary arts and interned at Hamersley's Bistro and Salamander Restaurant in Boston and at the Four Seasons in Atlanta. She has appeared on a Food Network TV show on cheese, is an expert on 350 cheeses, taught classes on the subject and was even greeted as the "cheese lady." She is now working as a buyer of domestic and imported cheeses for the Artisanal Cheese Center (www.artisanalcheese.com).

Kathy Hines is a graduate of the University of Texas at Austin and a student at the Wharton School at the University of Pennsylvania. She worked as an associate consultant at Bain and Company in Dallas and London and plans to work in general management at a Fortune 1000 company after graduating. She also enjoys exploring alternative leadership and emotional development initiatives and is a co-organizer of Leading From Within, a leadership seminar involving self-awareness and meditation. Her interests include cooking, fitness, board games and spending time with her husband and six-year-old daughter.

Saul A. Lopez is a graduate of the University of Illinois at Urbana-Champaign and a recent graduate of the Wharton School at the University of Pennsylvania, where he was a Howard Mitchell Fellowship recipient. Before business school, he worked as a consultant at Accenture in systems implementation and as a senior product manager at Usinternetworking, and he is now working at Nike as a senior business analyst in global operations. He is a competitive amateur cyclist and taught spinning classes at Wharton.

Juan Carlos Loredo received his bachelor's degree from the University of Texas and is a recent graduate of the McCombs School of Business at the University of Texas at Austin. At the age of 24, he became TruGreen LandCare's youngest branch manager, overseeing a $3.7 million division and reduced direct labor costs from 50 percent to less than 30 percent. He enjoys skiing and water-skiing and was a member of his college's jump team.

Fernando Maddock is a graduate of Lehigh University and a recent graduate of Dartmouth's Tuck School of Business, where he was a Consortium for Graduate Study in Management Fellow. Prior to Tuck, he worked as an analyst for a boutique investment bank focused exclusively on Latin American M&A, strategic advisory services and private equity. Since graduating from Tuck, Fernando has been taking some time off to enjoy life (recognizing that he will probably work for the rest of his life!) while also pursuing new business opportunities between the U.S. and Latin America.

Colby Maher received her B.A. in communications studies from UCLA and is a recent graduate of the Kellogg School of Management at Northwestern. She has worked for Accenture and eToys. Since graduating she has traveled in Central America to learn Spanish, volunteered and begun working at Booz Allen Hamilton in consulting.

Jeff Marquez received his bachelor's degree from UCLA and is a student at UCLA's Anderson School. He worked as a CRM manager and principle consultant at Pricewaterhouse Coopers, where he managed a 10-person team in deploying Siebel Systems software to more than 1,000 users in 10 countries, and as a senior business analyst at Scient. Jeff is also the president of Anderson's Latin Management Student Association and a member of the Screen Actors Guild, having appeared in commercials and print advertisements.

Donald C. Martin is the associate dean for enrollment at the University of Chicago Graduate School of Business. He is a member of the Graduate Management Admission Council and has written articles for various business publications.

Rosemaria Martinelli is the director of MBA admissions and financial aid at the Wharton School at the University of Pennsylvania. Rose received both her undergraduate and Master's degrees in music from Northwestern University and spent the first 15 years of her career as a professional opera singer.

Patrick J. McGinnis is a graduate of the Georgetown School of Foreign Service and a student at the Harvard Business School. While at Georgetown, he studied at the Universidad Torcuato di Tella in Buenos Aires, Argentina, as a Rotary Ambassadorial Scholar. Patrick began his career in the Latin America group at Chase Securities before joining JPMorgan Partners. As a private equity associate, he was appointed to the board of directors of Hispanic Teleservices Corporation. Patrick has been the director of Sursum Corda, a literacy program for elementary school children in Washington, D.C., and has lobbied on Capitol Hill to support student financial aid. He plans to work in private equity after graduation.

Colleen McMullen-Smith is the associate director of MBA admissions and career services at Carnegie Mellon University.

Martin Morgades is a graduate of the University of Texas at Austin and a recent graduate of the Jones Graduate School of Management at Rice University. He has worked as a legislative aide for the Texas Senate and for the El Paso Energy Corporation. Martin also played soccer professionally in Europe. He is now working in commercial real estate with a Real Estate Investment Trust.

Kristina L. Nebel is the director of admissions and financial aid at the University of Michigan Business School. She is a board member of the Consortium for Graduate Study in Management, serves on the steering committee for the Business School's Women in Business Initiative and is an executive board member for the Forté Foundation, a new nonprofit organization focused on women in business. She has a Master's in resource policy and administration from the University of Michigan and a bachelor's in mechanical engineering from Penn State University.

Lisa C. Olmos is a graduate of Harvard University and a student at both Rice's Jones Graduate School of Management and Baylor College of Medicine in Houston, Texas. After graduating, she plans to complete her medical training and use her MBA to advocate for a better healthcare system. A native of Washington, DC, she is also an avid competitive swimmer.

Leticia Pearman is a graduate of Cornell University and a recent graduate of the Kellogg School of Management at Northwestern. Before business school, she was an economic consultant at Grant Thornton in New York City. She is now a manager in the strategy and analytics group of Digitas, a marketing consulting firm specializing in customer relationship management programs for clients in Boston.

Valerie R. Ramirez received her B.A. from the University of California at Berkeley and Master's in public administration at Columbia University. She is a student at the Wharton School at the University of Pennsylvania. Before business school, she worked for several years for a U.S. Congressman in California as his campaign manager and Congressional Aide. In addition to this, Valerie also worked as a strategy consultant with IBM Consulting advising government clients on e-commerce applications. She was the second member of her family (her older brother was first) to complete her college degree and became the first in her family to obtain a graduate degree.

Abdiel A. Santiago is a graduate of the University of Denver and a recent graduate Northwestern's Kellogg School of Management. He plans to work in investment banking.

Ruben Sigala is a graduate of the University of Kansas and a recent graduate of the Harvard Business School. Before business school, he worked as a senior consultant in the financial services industry.

Paul Todgham received his B.A. from Harvard University and a Master's in economics at Cambridge University. He is a student at the Stanford Graduate

School of Business and was named a Siebel scholar in recognition of his academic performance and leadership. Before business school, Paul worked as a management consultant for the Boston Consulting Group developing strategies for clients in high technology and financial services. He spent his summer internship working for Microsoft, assisting the company with its strategy in security software. Outside of school, Paul pursues a range of outdoor activities, including hiking, sailing and whitewater kayaking. He attributes this passion for the outdoors to his Canadian upbringing and 14 summers of camp in Ontario.

Wenny Tung received an undergraduate degree from the University of Delaware, a Master's in corporate communications and technology from Rollins College and an MBA at the Fuqua School of Business at Duke. Before business school she worked in sales and operations at Walt Disney World, and she also interned in brand marketing at Johnson & Johnson. She is now working in brand marketing for the Disneyland Resort brand.

Juan Uribe is a graduate of Cornell University and a recent graduate of the Harvard Business School. Before business school, he worked as a management consultant at First Manhattan Consulting Group, a firm that specializes in financial services. He now works for Boston Consulting Group.

Consortium for Graduate Study in Management

5585 Pershing Avenue, Suite 240
St. Louis, MO 63112
www.cgsm.org
The CGSM Fellowship is for MBA study at a member school. Applicants must be U.S. Citizens and members of one of the following minority groups: African-American, Hispanic American or Native American. The fellowship covers full tuition and fees.

National Society of Hispanic MBAs

scholarships@nshmba.org
www.nshmba.org
The National Society of Hispanic MBAs provides financial aid to Latino students working towards a Master's degree in management/business. Applicants must be of Hispanic background, must be U.S. Citizens or Legal Permanent Residents and must be accepted into a graduate management/business major at an accredited college or university. Scholarships are awarded upon evaluation of academic achievement, contribution to the community, financial need, letters of recommendation and an essay.

Future Business Leaders of America–Phi Beta Lambda

www.fbla-pbl.org
FBLA-PBL is a non-profit organization that prepares students for careers in business. The organization has four divisions: FBLA Middle Level for junior high students, FBLA for high school students, PBL for postsecondary students and the Professional Alumni Division for business people, educators and parents.

About the Authors

Harvard graduates and husband and wife team, Gen and Kelly Tanabe are the founders of SuperCollege and the award-winning authors of nine books including *1001 Ways to Pay for College, Get Free Cash for College, How to Write a Winning Scholarship Essay, Get into Any College* and *Accepted! 50 Successful College Admission Essays.*

Gen and Kelly give workshops at colleges across the country and write the nationally syndicated "Ask the SuperCollege Experts" column. They have made hundreds of appearances on television and radio and have served as expert sources for respected publications including *USA Today, The New York Times,* the *New York Daily News,* the *San Jose Mercury News, U.S. News & World Report,* the *Chronicle of Higher Education* and *CNN.*

For this book Gen and Kelly interviewed dozens of students who were accepted by selective business school programs. They also met with admission officers to learn what happens behind the closed doors of the admission office.

Gen, Kelly and their son Zane live in Belmont, California.